Ecobehavioral Family Interventions in Developmental Disabilities

Ecobehavioral Family Interventions in Developmental Disabilities /

John R. Lutzker

University of Judaism

Randy Campbell

Behavior Change Associates

Brooks/Cole Publishing Company
Pacific Grove, California

I T P ™
The trademark ITP is used under license.

Brooks/Cole Publishing Company
A Division of Wadsworth, Inc.

Printed in the United States of America

10 9 8 7 6 5 4 3 2 1

Library of Congress Cataloging-in-Publication Data
Lutzker, John R., [date]
　　Ecobehavioral family interventions in developmental disabilities /
John R. Lutzker, Randy Campbell.
　　　　p.　cm.
　　Includes bibliographical references and index.
　　ISBN 0-534-24396-7
　　　1. Developmentally disabled—Family relationships.　2. Family
social work.　3. Social ecology.　I. Campbell, Randy.　II. Title.
　HV1570.L87　1994
　362.19'68—dc20　　　　　　　　　　　　　　　　　94-3954
　　　　　　　　　　　　　　　　　　　　　　　　　　　　CIP

Sponsoring Editor: *Vicki Knight*
Editorial Associate: *Lauri Banks Ataide*
Production Editor: *Nancy L. Shammas*
Production Service: *Scratchgravel Publishing Services*
Manuscript Editor: *Kay Mikel*
Permissions Editor: *Carline Haga*
Interior Design: *Roy R. Neuhaus*
Cover Design: *Susan Haberkorn*
Typesetting: *Scratchgravel Publishing Services*
Printing and Binding: *Malloy Lithographing, Inc.*

About the Authors

John R. Lutzker received his Ph.D. in developmental and child psychology from the Department of Human Development and Family Life at the University of Kansas. Currently, he is the Florence and Louis Ross Professor and chair of the Department of Psychology, Lee College, University of Judaism. Concurrently, he is a clinical associate professor of pediatrics, California College of Medicine, University of California, Irvine, and adjunct professor of human development, University of Kansas. He is also president of Behavior Change Associates. Dr. Lutzker is a fellow of the American Psychological Association, the American Psychological Society, and the American Association of Applied and Preventive Psychology.

Randy Campbell received his Rh.D. (Doctor of Rehabilitation) from the Rehabilitation Institute, Southern Illinois University, Carbondale. Currently, he is associate professor of education, Division of Administration and Counseling, California State University, Los Angeles. Concurrently, he is program manager, Behavior Change Associates/Project Ecosystems. He is also president of the Association for Behavior Analysis and Therapy/ Southern California.

Contents

CHAPTER FIVE
Stress Reduction 47

CHAPTER SIX
Counseling and Problem Solving 56

CHAPTER SEVEN
Behavioral Pediatrics 67

CHAPTER ELEVEN
Ethical Issues 107

Preface

This book describes an ecobehavioral model we have been using for more than 15 years with families involved in child abuse and neglect and with families who have children with developmental disabilities. We have recently extended the model for use with adults with developmental disabilities and dual diagnosis, for clients with head injury, and for adults with chronic schizophrenia.

The purposes of this book are fourfold: to describe the historical and research context for the model; to describe the service/treatment components of the model as we use them in our work on Project Ecosystems; to describe the application of the model to families who have children with developmental disabilities; and to raise questions regarding evaluation and issues of ethical concern when working with this and similar programs.

This book can be used as a manual for professionals and agencies interested in replicating the model, as a resource for professionals working in developmental disabilities and related fields, and as a reference/textbook for courses in special education, psychology, social work, counseling, and rehabilitation.

Chapter 1 begins with a review and explanation of the ecobehavioral approach. Chapter 2 reviews the precedents for social ecological approaches in psychology and special education. Chapter 3 provides an overview of the history and development of Project Ecosystems. Specific coverage of the service components offered by Project Ecosystems follow and include parent/child relationship training (Chapter 4), stress reduction (Chapter 5), counseling and problem solving (Chapter 6), and behavioral pediatrics (Chapter 7). Chapter 8 covers basic skills training for children.

Each of these chapters contains case examples from Project Ecosystems. In all circumstances, the names used in case examples are pseudonyms. Most of the case examples are actual verbatim examples; a few represent composite examples from families served by Project Ecosystems.

Chapter 9 covers staff training, an essential element of the ecobehavioral model. Chapter 10 stresses the role of systematic evaluation methods for this and similar human service projects. Finally, Chapter 11 deals with the ethical issues involved in providing an ecobehavioral service model.

Throughout this book we use terms from behavioral psychology, assuming a very basic knowledge by the reader. Any reader unfamiliar with terms such as *positive reinforcement, shaping, time-out,* and so on, is referred to any number of excellent texts covering the basic concepts of behavioral psychology and applied behavior analysis.

Acknowledgments

Several people deserve our gratitude. First and foremost is Dr. Kim B. Huynen, the other program manager for Project Ecosystems. Kim has served on the project since its inception, first as a graduate assistant, later as a counselor, and finally as a colleague. She is a creative clinician, a superior supervisor, and a trusted colleague. Thank you, Kim.

Next, the entire staff of Project 12-Ways during our southern Illinois years deserve our appreciation. They were with us as we struggled in the beginning, trying to put together the ecobehavioral model, and much of the success of the project was due to their creativity and diligence, not to mention the thousands of miles driving through rural southern Illinois in all kinds of weather.

Our current staff of Project Ecosystems could hardly be a nicer, more dedicated group of professionals. They have to drive thousands of miles of crowded freeways and rural desert roads. We truly almost never hear a complaint from them, and we receive frequent accolades from families and agency personnel because of their excellent service to our clients.

We work with many helpful agency personnel; however, three professionals deserve special mention. Elaine Bamberg, Director of the Developmental Disabilities Center of Orange County; Harry Taylor; and Phil Guardabascio have been constantly supportive, creative, and helpful in putting Project Ecosystems together and keeping it alive during strained financial times.

We are thankful to the following reviewers for their insightful comments: Jennifer Kilgo, Virginia Commonwealth University; and Linda Thurston, Kansas State University.

Clerical support has been provided by Randi Sherman, and other production support has been provided by Hilary Taub and Joan Cochrane; Vicki Knight, Lauri Banks Ataide, and Nancy Shammas of Brooks/Cole; and Anne Draus of Scratchgravel. Dr. Paul Touchette has helped us professionally in countless ways. He is a very special colleague for whom we have the utmost regard. Matthew Sher has provided helpful legal advice and friendship.

Finally, our love and appreciation is extended to our wives, Sandra and Mary; and to our children, Dov and Tov, and Maggie and Brian. They make it all worthwhile.

John R. Lutzker
Randy Campbell

CHAPTER ONE

The Ecobehavioral Approach

Tidepools Are Like Families

Marine biologists study tidepools because they are circumscribed environments. Every organism in a tidepool affects the ecology of the tidepool, and
any change in the ecology of the tidepool affects every organism living in
it. What does a tidepool have to do with a family? A family shares many of
the characteristics of the tidepool. That is, each family creates a social ecology. Within that social ecology, each family member affects the others. And,
as with tidepools, other changes in the social ecology affect the individuals
within the family. Thus, the "eco" in ecobehavioral represents the view that
a family is a social ecology. To provide an example of this social ecology,
we will describe a fictional family, the Andersons, a composite of many
families with children with developmental disabilities.

1

Dave Anderson, age 37, is a self-employed plumber. He is a high school graduate who attended one year of community college. His wife, Cynthia Anderson, age 37, is trained as a bookkeeper. She holds an A.A. degree from a community college. Currently, Cynthia works at home, providing bookkeeping services for a few small businesses and earning around $10,000 per year. The family lives in a three-bedroom home in a suburban community. The Andersons have two children, Adrian, a 7-year-old girl of normal intelligence who attends second grade in a public school, and Sean, a 5-year-old boy with severe mental retardation. From 9:00 A.M. to 12:30 P.M. each week day, Sean attends a developmental center preacademic program operated by the county. Sean is not toilet trained. He has some receptive language but is frequently noncompliant. He has an expressive vocabulary limited to *yes, no, Daddy, Mommy, Adee* (Adrian), *kool* (school), *car, kanee* (candy), and *owside* (outside). He becomes mildly self-injurious by biting his hand whenever demands are placed upon him. He interacts very little with peers; Sean's primary interactions with his sister involve aggression.

Prior to Adrian's birth, Cynthia worked full time for an accounting firm, earning over $40,000 per year. When Adrian was born, Cynthia reduced her work to half time and planned to continue on that basis when Sean was born. However, when Sean was 13 months old, some of his delays began to become apparent. He seemed to take more time from Cynthia than Adrian had. Thus, the Andersons decided that Cynthia would stay home with Sean. The Andersons were a happy couple earning a manageable income. However, as Sean has grown so have problems within the family.

Adrian had been excited at the prospect of a baby brother, as many older sisters are. In Sean's first year, Adrian often assisted her mother in diapering, bathing, and feeding Sean. She also enjoyed entertaining him. Now, Adrian has developed a behavior problem, often expressing a lack of understanding as to why her brother receives more attention from her parents and why he is "allowed" to behave in ways they would not tolerate from her. As a result, Adrian has become noncompliant and often whines.

Dave and Cynthia have begun to have marital problems. Their problems revolve around two issues: child discipline and money. Dave believes that Cynthia is too lenient with both children. He contends that he has little difficulty controlling their behavior and that if Cynthia would only imitate his practices she would not have problems controlling their behavior.

Dave's approach to the children is to yell loudly at them and spank Sean when he is noncompliant or aggressive. Because Dave spends far less time with the children than Cynthia does, these strategies appear to work for him. Yelling at Adrian and spanking Sean usually suppress any ongoing behavior at the moment but has done little to correct the behavior problems over time. In fact, his techniques have probably exacerbated the children's behavior problems.

Cynthia has expressed her concern to Dave that he has been hitting Sean more frequently and harder. She is truly concerned that he will cause permanent physical or psychological harm to Sean. Because of these serious disagreements over their respective child-rearing practices, Dave spends less time around the house than before, causing additional tension between the couple.

With their income reduced and Dave's business not as economically healthy as it once was, financial concerns add considerable tension for the family. Dave has asked Cynthia to return to her previous job, but she has been unable to find acceptable arrangements for Sean and is not certain she wants to find an all-day placement for him. Cynthia would feel neglectful and guilty leaving Sean in someone else's care for the entire day.

Finally, the family has become more insular. They used to enjoy trips together to malls, to movies, on drives, to pizza parlors, and occasionally to amusement parks. They had a number of friends and visited the couple's parents on alternating weekends (Dave's parents one weekend and Cynthia's parents the next weekend). Most of the activities have diminished or have been eliminated entirely, largely because of Sean's behavior but recently also because Adrian is less pleasant than she used to be.

In creating the Andersons, we have tried to paint a picture of the issues of social ecology and, in doing so explain the "eco" in ecobehavioral. Our focus, as you will see throughout this book, is on treating the ecosystem issues rather than seeing Sean's noncompliance as a singular problem.

Components of the Ecobehavioral Approach

The "behavioral" in ecobehavioral represents the methodology. The behavioral methodology is a focus on direct observation of behavior in situ: that is, we observe and treat behavior in the settings in which the challenging behaviors occur. Thus, if the Andersons have difficulty taking the children to a shopping mall or a video store, we will observe their interactions in these environments and provide direct behavioral strategies for solving challenging behavior in these settings.

By observation, we mean that formal data are collected by a counselor, and sometimes by two counselors at the same time. The most common data collection technique is interval recording. This method involves breaking the observation sessions, such as a trip to the grocery store, into smaller intervals, usually 30 seconds or one minute. The observer then records the occurrence or nonoccurrence of one or more behaviors within however many one-minute or 30-second intervals there are during the sessions. This data collection technique allows for fairly accurate behavioral observations.

Planned activities and incidental teaching are appropriate for going to the mall, but behavioral relaxation training may be appropriate for going to the dentist. With the tension the parents are currently experiencing, we might also use relaxation procedures with Dave and Cynthia in teaching them how to be patient with the parent training procedures to which we are exposing them. We adopt whatever procedures are appropriate to the situation and to the individual behavioral dynamics of the family.

Whenever possible, a single-subject research design is used as part of the methodology. This means that reliability observers are used at least 25 percent of the time and that a multiple baseline design is employed to ensure empirical confidence that the changes in behavior can clearly be seen to be a function of the training procedures. Planned activities training has been found to be at least as effective as contingency management training (Harrold, Lutzker, Campbell, & Touchette, 1992). Withdrawal single-subject research designs have been of little use in our work because most of the behaviors we teach to parents and their children are neither practically nor ethically reversible.

Developmental issues also represent an aspect of the ecobehavioral approach. Treatment strategies must balance two developmental concerns. They must match the developmental skill level of the individual, and they should never be demeaning or nonfunctional. For example, Sean would benefit from functional communication training that begins with the recognition that he has few language skills. At the same time, it is important to be sure he is taught only *functional* skills at the present time. Teaching him farm animal sounds, something we have observed teachers and parents of special needs children doing, would be inappropriate at Sean's current level of functioning. He needs to learn to say "please" and "I want" and to practice some preacademic skills.

A component we describe as a resource specialist also represents an aspect of the ecobehavioral model. In the case of the Andersons, a counselor might advise them to seek respite care from the regional center for their children so they could take a vacation for a weekend to celebrate their tenth wedding anniversary. Or it might involve giving the Andersons a list of books that would be appropriate to read to Sean.

The ecobehavioral model also includes a biobehavioral component. Behavioral methodology can be used to monitor the effects of psychotropic medications, such as methylphenidate. It can also be used to help a family with compliance to medication. For example, Sean has a calcium deficiency and is required to take medication he appears to dislike. Counselors could teach the family how to "fade in" the necessary amount of liquid medication in ice cream and how to set up a simple reinforcement system for Sean's compliance in taking his medication. Biobehavioral approaches can be useful in the treatment of attention deficit hyperactive disorder (ADHD). For example, Pelham and Hinshaw (1992) suggest that physicians should seek consultation from behavioral psychologists when evaluating the behavioral effects of medication aimed at treating ADHD.

Finally, generalization programming is an important aspect of the ecobehavioral model. For any treatment program to be successful, active programming for generalization across time, behaviors, and settings is necessary (Stokes & Baer, 1977). As will be seen in Chapter 4, in which we more fully describe planned activities training, programming across settings and time is a major component of the parent training program.

The clearest set of guidelines for actively promoting generalization is provided by Stokes and Baer (1977). They offer a number of strategies to increase the likelihood that generalization will occur, and it is important to be aware of these strategies and to use them as much as possible. For example, with a family such as the Andersons, we would advise them that as many individuals as are relevant and willing should participate in the planned activities and other behavior management training strategies. In the Anderson family, we would ask both parents to be involved, and we would include Adrian. If there is a regular babysitter, we might include that individual in training also. Similarly, we would conduct parent/child skill training in several settings.

In working with Sean's communication skills, we would teach them in functional settings. For example, we would teach "I want (the name of a food or drink) in the kitchen and in the living room and at the mall. We might teach "up" or "down" on a teeter-totter and use the natural consequence of up or down as the activity reinforcer for the communication skill.

In teaching the family planned activities and incidental teaching in the supermarket, different stores would be used. Similarly, to prompt Cynthia to remember to use some of the techniques she was taught during training at home in trips to the market, we might ask her to wear a red ribbon around her wrist and to prompt communication with Sean at home. Now, we would ask her to also wear the ribbon when taking Sean to the store.

Using generalization strategies increases the likelihood of producing generalization with parents and their children. Stokes and Baer (1977) coined the phrase *train and hope*. Unless active "promotional" strategies are used to produce generalization, those who provide training merely hope for generalization to occur. We have found that using generalization strategies almost always avoids having to rely solely on hope.

The Historical Context

The late 1960s were marked by significant changes in treatment approaches and outcomes in psychology and related fields. Behavior modification and behavior therapy techniques were showing that serious problems, such as severe phobias and autism, could be responsive to treatments based largely on the principles of operant and respondent conditioning. Needless to say, however, behavioral approaches were not without critics. Those who observed these techniques in use with individuals with developmental disabilities were concerned that the procedures appeared mechanical and that some of the outcomes also appeared mechanical. For example, in treating children with autism, while their language often clearly improved, it sounded robot-like and little or no spontaneous language was observed.

Only in the 1980s and 1990s were these concerns addressed. More naturalistic teaching strategies and more naturalistic reinforcers were used; even some of the child's very peculiarities were used as reinforcers, such as a child's particular perseverative item or self-stimulation (Charlop, Kurtz, & Casey, 1990).*

In the early 1970s several ecological psychologists suggested that behavioral psychologists needed to pay more attention to the effect of their treatments on the child's broader ecology. For example, to treat a problem such as a nervous tic in an office or home would ignore the many other settings in which children behave. Also, it would be worth investigating how other children reacted to the tic. Did they make fun of it, or did it provide attention the child otherwise would not receive? If the latter were the case and some kind of social skill were not taught in the absence of the tic, it is possible that eliminating the tic would cause the child to have fewer social interactions or to develop another inappropriate behavior to receive the attention that was provided in response to the tic.

Thus, in a series of responses and rebuttals (Rogers-Warren & Warren, 1977), some constructive suggestions occurred between ecological psychology and what had come to be known as applied behavior analysis (the socially relevant application of the laboratory principles of operant conditioning). This led to recognition that there was a need in applied behavior analysis to examine as many variables as practical when observing and treating challenging child behavior. Further, the effects of treatment should be examined in as many settings in which the child interacts as possible, and their effect on others within the child's social ecology—such as parents, teachers, and peers—should also be examined.

Although this discussion was provocative in the 1970s, it was not until the 1980s that research began to appear from this ecobehavioral perspective. Of course, an ecobehavioral approach represents quite a deviation from a normal clinical, office-based model. And this new perspective was clearly more expensive and more time-consuming than other models. Logic would dictate, however, that the approach might have better long-term benefits than more traditional models.

An example of the need to recognize parental issues in the treatment of children with developmental disabilities was provided in research conducted by Black, Molaison, and Smull (1990). They found that as children become older, parental requests for placement were related to family stressors. The more stress the family experienced, the more likely it was that the family would request placement. Black et al. (1990) suggest that attending

---

Perseveration is a technical term for one of the idiosyncrasies often seen in autism. A child with autism may *perseverate* on an object, literally anything, to a point of obsession. For example, one child's perseverative item was a particular brand and model of car. On his own, he would spend all his time thumbing through catalogs of that car. During language training sessions, access to the pictures in the catalogs was made contingent on attending behavior and correct language responses.

to ecobehavioral issues such as family support reduces the likelihood of a request for placement. Similarly, Dyson (1991) suggested that treatment programs for families with children with developmental disabilities should be individually tailored to the families' needs and that attention should be paid to relieving stressors in the families' ecosystems.

Roberts, Wasik, Casto, and Ramey (1991) have pointed to the need to address several of the issues representing an ecobehavioral approach. They suggest that treatment must be in situ, that intervention must occur at minimum on a weekly basis, and that treatment must focus on the family rather than only on a "target" child. Further, they point to Project 12-Ways (Lutzker, 1984), an ecobehavioral predecessor to Project Ecosystems that dealt with families involved in child abuse and neglect, as an example of the kind of community-based program that begins to address these broad-based concerns.

Similarly, Hutchins and McPherson (1991) have noted that delivery systems must be flexible, accessible, and responsive to family needs and that *developmental* issues must be a focus of intervention services. Roberts and Magrab (1991) add to these concerns that services must be family-centered and community-based. Further, they note that services must account for and treat the family's social ecology and that care should be interdisciplinary (such as biobehavioral). They also reinforce the need to take a developmental perspective. Roberts and Magrab (1991) point out that services should not assess and treat families in the abstract: "time would not be spent in formal assessment but in such mundane chores as going to the supermarket..., or helping with feeding or bathing a child who is quadriplegic" (p. 147). They rue the fact that few training programs teach staff or students family development, infant assessment, or ecological approaches to assessment and intervention.

Community-Based Programs

Project Ecosystems, described in detail in Chapter 3, is hardly the only community-based approach to treating families with children with developmental disabilities. It is, however, an outgrowth of a community-based philosophy along with a social ecological philosophy. Zigler, Hodapp, and Edison (1990) remind us that issues and solutions to the care and education of individuals with mental retardation swing on a historical pendulum. Philosophy and attitude about services play a role, but so do political, economic, and social issues. Recently, economics has probably played the strongest role.

In the United States, the move to the community was launched in 1972 with Wolfsenberger's *The Principle of Normalization in Human Services*. This has come to mean that in the provision of community services the environments in which services are provided should be as normal as possible (Zigler et al., 1990). And programs aimed at teaching functional community skills should produce normalization. The in-home, in-situ approach of Project Ecosystems is in "synch" with this philosophy. Further, Zigler et al. (1990) suggested was that services should be matched to the developmental level of the client, something we have tried to stress as an aspect of our ecobehavioral model.

Community-based approaches grew out of philosophical and policy concerns; however, they also make eminent sense from a behavioral perspective. We know it is best to try to change behavior in the setting in which the challenging behaviors occur. An in-situ approach seems to be the most logical approach from an ethical, practical treatment perspective. Also, the repeated theme of the need to put developmental issues into perspective makes common sense from a behavioral perspective. Doing so is practical and means that a child is taught skills that are most likely to be maintained in the natural environment.

A strong argument for the need to adapt treatment programs to the natural environment has been made by Gregg and Williamson (1992). They note that even today many behavior management procedures are laboratory-based and trained. These procedures may not be adaptable to the complicated lives of families with children who have developmental disabilities.

Summary

The ecobehavioral approach described in this book focuses on the family as an ecosystem. Treatment is based on dealing directly with the challenges within that ecosystem. The ecobehavioral model actively programs for generalization and is critically aware of developmental issues.

The entire Anderson family would be involved in an ecobehavioral service. The parents and Adrian would learn how to teach Sean new skills and how to help him maintain those skills. The parents would receive training in problem solving and stress reduction. Developmental concerns would be of paramount importance to assure a balance between teaching Sean skills that are not above his current ability to perform while making sure that any new skills taught are not demeaning but functional. Assessment and treatment would occur in the multiple settings in which the family normally interacts, and assessments would go beyond the obvious needs of Sean to measures of family satisfaction with each other and with the services provided.

A rationale for an ecobehavioral perspective has been provided by professionals who have called for approaches that treat the individual within his or her social environment. A concern has been expressed that services to families who have children with developmental disabilities must be in situ and *practical*. Further, all family members need some attention from the professionals serving them; treatment cannot be focused solely on the child with developmental disabilities.

CHAPTER TWO

A Social Ecological Perspective

The Anderson family represents only one of a constellation of different and differing family social ecologies. Most of this book describes our work on Project Ecosystems, an ecobehavioral approach to treating families who have children with developmental disabilities. The families we see in Project Ecosystems represent countless differing social ecologies. Singer and Irvin (1989) have said, "For many purposes, a multifaceted view of the family is necessary in order to recognize the complexity and uniqueness of each family" (p. 16). This chapter will present what others have described when examining social ecologies in developmental disabilities and will relate their work to our own at Project Ecosystems.

Two of the pioneers in the recognition of social ecologies among families with children with developmental disabilities are Ann and Rudd Turnbull. Their book, *Families, Professionals, and Exceptionality: A Special*

Partnership (1990), details these issues in depth. Here, we will try to provide a brief overview of their work.

The Turnbulls point out the changing historical role of parents when dealing with developmental disabilities, both the view of their role in the procreation of children with developmental disabilities and their changing and changed roles in recent history in dealing with their children and society's response to them. One of the most stigmatizing and damaging events of the past 200 years for families involved in developmental disabilities was the "eugenics movement" (1880–1930). Most of this movement was a function of Goddard's 1912 study of the Kallikak family (Lutzker, 1993a). Goddard described a businessman who fathered a family by his wife and for whom all of the children were intellectually normal. The man also fathered children by a woman with mental retardation to whom he was not married. Most of the progeny of this woman had mental retardation. As a function of this, laws were passed restricting marriages to persons with intellectual disabilities and requiring compulsory sterilization. This resulted in sharp increases in institutionalization of thousands of Americans with developmental disabilities and mental illness.

Major changes began to occur in the 1950s away from institutionalization and restriction of rights for people with developmental disabilities. Much of this change was a function of the work of the founders of what is now known as the Association for Retarded Citizens (ARC). In 1954, the first national headquarters was opened, and President Eisenhower declared the first National Retarded Children's Week (Turnbull & Turnbull, 1990). Between 1956 and 1961, there was a nearly 700 percent increase in funding for research and services in mental retardation.

In 1969, ARC opened its governmental affairs office in Washington, D.C. In 1974, the name was changed to the National Association for Retarded Citizens (NARC). In 1986, largely as a result of the efforts of NARC, 11 major laws were enacted by the U.S. Congress, including the Education of the Handicapped Act Amendments.

During the 20th century, a range of change—from the eugenics scare to the 1986 and 1992 acts of Congress—has increased the rights of individuals with handicaps and disabilities. And the role of parents has also changed greatly. Because of the role of parents in groups such as NARC and in many other efforts, parents have become active participants in developing services for their young children and their adult children. This has included establishing programs in public schools, local community organizations, group homes, vocational services, and recreational services. Similarly, parents' roles have changed from being the passive recipients of professional recommendations about how to deal with their children, such as the too often ill-informed recommendation to institutionalize their children, to being very active participants in the provision of services to their children. Project Ecosystems counselors are taught *always* to have the parents participate actively in development of our treatment programs. As well, whenever possible the children also participate in development of their programs. Using the ecobehavioral model, it would be impossible not to have parents as the primary partners in development of treatment programs. Also, as will be seen in Chapter 6 on counseling and problem solving, we often guide parents to help them take a more active role with schools, agencies, and regional centers to improve the services their children receive.

The methodology and procedures of behavioral psychology and the ecobehavioral approach necessarily enroll parents as teachers and "learners" in development and implementation of treatment programs (Turnbull & Turnbull, 1990). When we feel we have failed a family served by Project Ecosystems, it is usually because we have failed to convince the parents of their need to participate in the program. Some parents carry an expectation that services will be provided by us and that they can back away from involvement with their children. Fortunately, such cases are rare.

Variables That Can Affect the Family Ecosystem

Parent training must be hands-on and should be in-home. For example, Bakken, Miltenberger, and Schauss (1993) found that parents with mental retardation who received training in a clinic expanded their *knowledge* about parent training but could not display parent training skills until those skills were taught directly in their homes. That these parents had mental retardation seems to us less relevant than the issue of the importance of in-home training to maximize the skills parents learn. *Intensive* early child and parent training has shown remarkable gains over the years with children with autism (McEachin, Smith, & Lovaas, 1993).

Among the roles parents have come to play is the role of political advocate. Without such advocacy, the already limited funds available for research and service would be considerably more limited. Similarly, parents have become what Turnbull and Turnbull (1990) have called "educational decision makers." Thus, parents have lobbied successfully for the rights to education for all children. As a part of this, it has been mandated that parents must take part in school-developed individual education plans (IEPs). As will be seen in case examples in subsequent chapters, our counselors frequently assist parents in preparing for IEP meetings at schools. Also, it is not infrequent that our counselors accompany the parents to these meetings.

Turnbull and Turnbull (1990) point out that family social ecologies can vary from the traditional family of two parents and their children to single parents (an increasing phenomenon, 40 percent of American families constitute a changed arrangement as a function of divorce). Also, in some families grandparents are actively involved or are living with the family. Siblings play a critical role, especially in families with children with developmental disabilities. As we saw with the Anderson family, an unusual burden is placed on the siblings of children with developmental disabilities. In fact, Breslau and Prabucki (1987) found that siblings of children with handicaps were more demoralized and aggressive than a control group of children. Further, at Project Ecosystems it is not unusual for us to see a family with more than one child with mental retardation or with twins with autism. Needless to say, this creates particular stress for parents. The quality of the marriage is clearly a variable in providing services to families, and it is well known that without good services marriages are especially strained when the child has or the children have disabilities.

Other variables that can affect the family ecosystem, how services are offered, and what their effects are include the characteristics of the child's exceptionality—that is, the severity and type of the disorder. These issues affect the demands placed on all family members.

In more than one place in this book, we will stress the need to be aware of and actively involved in adjusting services to accommodate cultural issues. We offer training to our staff members on the cultural differences of the dominant cultures we see in our service area (Caucasian, Hispanic, African American, Arab, Armenian, Asian). Turnbull and Turnbull (1990) offer a number of excellent suggestions for dealing with cultural issues, beginning with learning about other cultures. More specifically, learning about a culture's attitudes toward disabilities is very important. Just as differing cultures have different child-rearing practices, there are also differences in how they treat children with developmental disabilities.

Another suggestion in dealing with cultural differences is to actively solicit members of different cultural groups to participate in organizations as staff, board members, volunteers, and consultants. It is helpful to learn at least a few phrases of the different languages of the varying cultural groups served. This is a particular challenge in southern California, which is home to countless ethnic groups.

As we described in Chapter 1, acting as a resource specialist is a component of the ecobehavioral model. Thus, it is important to be knowledgeable about specific cultural groups' community activities, organizations, and resources. For example, we were serving an Armenian family in the San Fernando Valley, which has a large number of Armenians. The parents felt socially isolated dealing with their son who had Down syndrome and also trying to cope with the sibling issues of his two intellectually normal brothers. In addition to providing parent training and other Project Ecosystems services, we helped the family find an Armenian babysitter who had some experience with children with special needs. We also suggested that the parents join a social group at the Armenian Community Center. By hiring the babysitter, the parents were able to attend the social functions at the community center. They subsequently reported that they were more relaxed about the training we were offering them because they finally had some time for themselves to socialize with other adults from their own culture.

Hiring members of minority groups is an important and worthwhile goal. It also turns out to be easier said than done. Trained members of minority groups in southern California are in such demand that they are difficult to find. We have found it quite useful to advertise in campus newspapers and especially in minority group newspapers on campuses. (We hire only graduate and undergraduate students for our counseling staff). We have also found that once it is known to our referral sources that we have a staff member of a particular racial or ethnic group, that individual has more referrals than can possibly be handled. One of the long-term solutions to this problem is for graduate programs in behavior analysis and special education to more actively solicit and admit minority students to their programs.

Geographic location certainly affects services delivered to families. In general, rural communities receive fewer and often less competent professional services than do urban communities; yet, serving an urban community presents its own problems. Project Ecosystems serves urban, suburban, and rural communities. Traffic affects our counselors' abilities to schedule and deliver services in a timely manner. Some neighborhoods are outright dangerous, making it difficult for counselors to provide service to them. Although traffic is less of a problem in rural communities, distance is often a variable for the family and the service provider. Also, in rural communities ancillary services might be less available and of lesser quality. For example, Project Ecosystems served a family with a girl with autism and cerebral palsy. In addition to these disabilities, she had some serious opthomalogic problems. The pediatric opthamologist in the rural desert town in which she lived had no experience in testing children with developmental disabilities. Fortunately, with our contacts with a large university-affiliated hospital in Los Angeles, we were able to find a referral for the child to an eye specialist in a nearby neighboring community who had extensive experience with children with disabilities.

Other family ecological variables the Turnbulls suggest play a role in the ability to deliver service and in the families' practices with their children include the physical health of the family members, the parents' and siblings' coping styles, and certainly the socioeconomic status of the family. Biglan (1989) has pointed out that treating some of these issues involves defining and pursuing life goals through a problem-solving process, changing social behavior, and increasing activities.

Health problems of one or more family members can affect how they interact with the child with special needs and how able they are to follow through with training programs a project such as ours might suggest. As will be seen throughout this book, an ecobehavioral program involves considerable participation by the parents. Serious health problems can make the training difficult. We have found that stress reduction training for parents is a very helpful adjunct to the other services we offer, especially when health problems may be stress-related (see Chapter 5).

In addition to the health problems of family members, medication issues must be considered. Behavior analysts and behavioral psychologists are often loathe to accept the role biological factors may play in generating certain challenging behaviors. They are often unwilling to consider medication as an adjunct to behavioral treatment strategies. Medications may or may not be helpful in the treatment of challenging behavior. The ecobehavioral methodology can be used to assist in an in-situ functional analysis of whether a child is deriving benefits from a prescribed medication. That is, formal observations are conducted at home and in school to assess the effects of the medication. For example, we might be interested in the effects of pemoline (a psychostimulant used to treat ADHD) on challenging behavior at home and at school. For one month, baseline data would be collected on the child in these settings without the medication. Then, the child would be observed for six weeks in these settings when he or she was medicated. The medication would again be stopped for a month, and if the results showed clear improvements during the medicated period, the child would be placed back on the medication with continued follow-up observations.

As an example of etiology and treatment in behavioral pediatrics, Singh, Ricketts, Ellis, and Singh (1993) have suggested that self-injury may be related to the endogenous opoid system, with two nonexclusive mechanisms having been postulated to account for self-injurious behavior. In a related effort, Ricketts, Ellis, Singh, and Singh (1993) found that seven of nine studies showed a positive effect of naltrexone in the reduction of self-injury. Naltrexone improved measures of independence and attention and decreased trial rate in ten adolescent and adult residents of a developmental center (Taylor, Sandman, Touchette, Hetrick, & Barron, 1993). Chloropromizine and Thioridazine elevated discriminative performance for children with mental retardation (Beale, Smith, & Webster, 1993). Thus, medications may begin to play an increasingly important role in a broad-based ecobehavioral approach to treating individuals with developmental disabilities.

Children are at higher risk for abuse when they have disabilities, and they are at higher risk when they are poor. Many of the children seen by Project Ecosystems fit both of these categories. Thus, we are all the more concerned about having a positive impact in the family ecosystem, and we train our staff to be aware of the signs of abuse. Teaching a child many new self-help and social and communication skills goes a long way toward reducing risk factors, as does teaching stress reduction and problem-solving skills to the parents. Singer and Irvin (1989) have reported that the best predictor of maternal distress is the amount of help a child needs with the activities of daily living (ADLs). Thus, ensuring that new ADLs are taught to children with developmental disabilities is a critical aspect of any ecological/ecobehavioral approach.

Problems Associated with Delivery of In-Home Services

The in-home, in-situ nature of Project Ecosystems and similar projects produces additional burdens on families. Although service is, of course, designed to help families, service providers must be aware that time and energy are required by families to meet with counselors, receive training and counseling, and implement the programs. In fact, Wahler and Fox (1980) have suggested that when a parent is not having a "good day" no parent training should be attempted. Instead, on "bad days" a session can be devoted to more humanistic counseling strategies. We frequently remind our counselors of this and encourage them to evaluate the family status for the day during a counseling visit. Flexibility is of paramount concern in delivering these services.

Counseling visits and many of the other conflicts in family scheduling are variables that can affect the follow through and outcome of delivering services. We have found the problem-solving procedures described in Chapter 6 very useful in helping families cope with and arrange effective schedules with us and with the many activities and events in their lives that need organization and scheduling.

As we mentioned earlier, siblings are as affected as other members of the family ecosystem by a child with developmental disabilities. Turnbull and Turnbull (1990) have noted that siblings should not be expected to be saints. This is certainly the case. As Adrian Anderson clearly became disappointed and later jealous of her brother, many children become especially burdened by several aspects of their siblings' strange behavior in public or around their friends. Also, as was the case with the Andersons, the sibling may become jealous or lack understanding of the reason the child with disabilities receives special attention. Older children can be encouraged to join support groups for siblings; however, we have found that incorporating siblings into the teaching and training programs offered to the parents and to their brother or sister with the disability is very helpful in allaying some of these problems. Also, training can be provided to teach the child with the disability how to behave in a more adaptive manner with the intellectually normal sibling. Countless families who have received our planned activities training described in Chapter 4 have reported that they have found the procedures especially useful with their other children and that this has helped develop more family harmony.

As the siblings are included in the ecobehavioral training program, grandparents, family friends, other significant relatives, and in some homes, housekeepers must also be included. Without involving such important members of the family social ecology, treatment effects have a narrow outcome.

A similar outlook to the Turnbulls' has been expressed by Prinz (1992), who has suggested four necessary components of the behavioral aspect of ecobehavioral approaches to treating families. First, he stresses the importance of observable behavior. Data must be collected with families using direct observation methods that allow an objective interpretation of family interactions. Second, he also stresses the social environment, mentioning many of the issues also described by the Turnbulls. Third, Prinz notes that the use of natural change agents is a critical feature of this approach. That is, it makes little sense for counselors to teach skills or try to modify the challenging behaviors of our clients when it is parents, siblings, teachers, grandparents, and others in the family social ecology who ultimately must implement behavior change programs. Finally, Prinz suggests the need to reframe the locus of the problem. The term *target child* has become popular in describing work with children, but we never use this term as it is antithetical to an ecobehavioral perspective. Such a term implies that a child could somehow be the only source of a problem. From the ecobehavioral perspective, this is clearly not possible.

Preventing Developmental and Behavioral Problems

In addition to treatment, prevention is a very important consideration in looking at families. Sanders and Markie-Dadds (1992) have offered five suggestions for effective prevention: early identification of at-risk children; a closer examination of the relationship between parent and child problems; changing the nature of developmental advice required by parents; examining the interrelationships between different risk factors; and recruiting and engaging multidistressed families. Although these authors were speaking specifically of conduct disorders, these issues are also relevant for families with children with developmental disabilities.

Early identification of children at risk is a major issue in developmental disabilities. This begins as early as prenatal training for young single mothers with whom many developmental disorders can be prevented by training in maternal prenatal care and prenatal and postnatal training of these young mothers in child care. For example, Delgado and Lutzker (1988) taught young single parents how to recognize and care for the medical needs of their babies. Also, Lutzker, Lutzker, Braunling-McMorrow, and Eddleman (1987) taught young single mothers how to provide stimulation to their babies. Both of these programs help prevent developmental delays that can occur from a variety of environmental reasons such as fetal alcohol syndrome, nutritional deficits during pregnancy, failure to recognize and act upon serious medical problems of infants, or failure to provide a psychologically and cognitively stimulating environment to an infant.

An aspect of the ecobehavioral model that will become increasingly apparent throughout this book is the need to recognize and treat or refer for treatment any dysfunctional behaviors of the parents that may be contributing to the challenges in the child with delays who is the reason for the referral. Thus, to proceed with parent training for a mother who is clinically depressed without dealing with the mother's depression presents a poor prognosis for success with the parent training.

Providing age appropriate and developmentally appropriate information according to the child's specific disabilities is another prerequisite for working with families. Forehand and Wierson (1993) note that developmental factors have all too often been ignored in child behavior therapy. They stress the following considerations in offering treatment:

1. The cognitive capacity of the child must be assessed.
2. Behavioral treatment strategies must be congruent with the current level of the child's development.
3. The context of treatment must broaden to include primary sources of reinforcement at each developmental age.

It is equally important to give parents new information regarding development as the child matures and gains more skills. This is what we have called the resource specialist aspect of the ecobehavioral model.

Sanders and Markie-Dadds (1992) also describe the interrelationships of risk factors. This is another way of describing the social ecology. For example, unemployment, substance abuse, adult/adult marital or other relationships, religious beliefs, and cultural issues can all have a significant role in how plans are made to work with a family and what might be accomplished (Weisner, Beizer, & Stolze, 1991). In one case example at Project Ecosystems, we were seeing an Armenian family who began to have marital problems as a function of new economic problems. The father was a self-employed jeweler; when the economy in California turned "sour," he was forced out of business. These new marital problems began to seriously hamper the considerable progress that had been made in parent training. Because of the counselor's skills, the family was comfortable in revealing the marital and economic problems they were having. The counselor was then able to find an Armenian counselor to help the parents with their marital problems. The parents reported that prior to working with the Project Ecosystems counselor, they never would have considered nor accepted marital counseling. Because of the trust they developed with the Project Ecosystems counselor, they were quite willing to seek out the referral the counselor found for them.

Religious and spiritual issues have received little attention in psychology and developmental disabilities even though they play such a large role in everyday life. Religion in families of children with developmental delays was examined by Weisner et al. (1991). They found that religious parents were somewhat more family-oriented than nonreligious parents. Also, religious parents emphasized parental nurturance and believed that their child was an opportunity rather than a burden. Being aware of these kinds of issues and learning to assess them, perhaps even incorporating them into the treatment offered or the manner in which treatment is offered, represents another important step in looking at these important social ecological variables in treating families.

Other family stressors service providers should be aware of include behavior challenges of the child, nighttime disturbances, social isolation of the family and the child, adversity in the family, the multiplicity of the child's impairments, the child's health, problems with the child's appearance, and parental economic issues (Singer & Irvin, 1989).

Recruiting families from California's regional center system may be easier than recruiting the multidistressed families described by Sanders and Markie-Dadds (1992). The more multiples of stressors and the greater the dysfunction, the less likely the family will be to seek and receive the help they need. For example, although California's regional center system is available to all families regardless of economic circumstance, if the child has developmental disabilities and the parent is unemployed, abuses a substance, and has a limited education, the parent is less likely to seek services until some other agency such as a school or medical provider refers or reports the family because of serious challenges for the child or because of other risk factors.

Ecological Factors

Although discussing ecology in residential facilities, Meinhold and Mulick (1990) have pointed to some factors that also need to be considered in families and within their homes. They note that ecology involves both the social ecology we have been discussing here and the physical ecology. These authors suggest that staff/staff interactions should be suppressed in favor of more staff/client interactions. As will be seen in subsequent chapters in this book, we feel that interactions—that is, engagement between parents and the children whom we serve—is one of the most critical elements of success in implementing an ecobehavioral model.

The arrangement of furniture and adaptive equipment is important in residential facilities and homes. Children should be allowed to participate in the choice of furnishings and the arrangements of a room (Nezu, Nezu, & Gill-Weiss, 1992). We have often recommended rearrangements of sleeping situations, beds, seating in dining situations, and so forth to facilitate other direct training we offer. For example, if two siblings disrupt each other at the dinner table and have been seated next to each other, a simple yet effective suggestion is to have a parent sit between the two siblings. Similarly, we have suggested that special child-safe areas be arranged in homes. In these areas, nothing can be broken and thus cause the child to incur the parents' ire. Also, we have developed an assessment (Tertinger, Greene, & Lutzker, 1988) and training program (Tertinger, Greene, & Lutzker, 1984; Barone, Greene, & Lutzker, 1986) for home safety, and a program for home cleanliness (Watson-Perczel, Lutzker, Greene, & McGimpsey, 1988; Lutzker, 1990a). Finally, parents need to be taught what powerful models they are (Nezu et al., 1992). All too often a parent will whine to us that the child whines too much. Or a parent will complain that the child is aggressive, and when we ask how the parent tries to manage that she tells us that she spanks the child. These kinds of hypocrisies need to be pointed out diplomatically during active parent training.

Some of the social ecological issues we have presented here have been described by Singer and Irvin (1989) as supported family living. These are relatively permanent arrangements of socioenvironmental conditions that provide support for behavior. Without rearrangements of certain conditions, problems for families will remain unsolved. Singer, Irvine, and Irvin (1989) have noted that until recently behavioral parent training has operated at a far too microanalytic level to be effective in helping to solve the socioenvironmental conditions that prevent true supported living for families. The kinds of contextual variables addressed in the ecobehavioral model are critical in providing for a supported family living environment. Singer, Irvine, and Irvin (1989) have noted that poverty is often an impediment to successful parent training; however, Baker (1984) reported successful efforts working with poor urban parents of children with developmental disabilities. He suggests that the counseling relationships we have described here are essential before proceeding with parent training with poor families.

Similarly, Szykula, Fleischman, and Shilton (1982) made additions to behavioral parent training that included self-control training, frequent telephone contact with the counselors, and help with housing, legal, and medical problems. Also, Griest, Forehand, Rogers, Breiner, Furey, and Williams (1982) provided counseling to help mothers increase positive interactions in the community, improve marital communication, and achieve more realistic perceptions of expectations about their children. Using these kinds of efforts, Singer, Irvine, and Irvin (1989) created an ecobehavioral program for families called Support and Education for Families (Project SAEF). This program was similar to Project Ecosystems and provided direct service for case management, service linkages, and advocacy. Parents were taught coping skills and had support groups arranged. Behavioral marital therapy and individual treatment for depression were provided to parents who required these services. In addition, behavioral parent training was accomplished through clinic-based training backed up by in-home coaching.

The Behavioral Family Intervention (BFI) program is another ecobehavioral approach to families (Sanders, 1992). It is described as an ecological perspective involved in the treatment of conduct disorder, pain, chronic health problems, anxiety disorders, and learning difficulties. Sanders has pointed out that despite the encouraging data from BFI and other ecological approaches, research is needed with families who drop out of such treatments or who never present in the first place.

A more fine-tuned ecobehavioral approach will appear when we have studied much more about the social ecologies of families who have no need of treatment. Once we learn what distinguished their social ecologies from families who need treatment, we may be able to offer more advanced ecobehavioral treatments to families in need of them.

Summary

In this chapter we have examined the social ecological perspective in treating families who have children with developmental disabilities. We have reviewed the work of others who have expressed the need to examine these ecological factors in providing a comprehensive treatment model. These authors have suggested considering siblings, significant others, housekeepers, and grandparents, among others, whenever a family receives services. Also, religion and spirituality is often a neglected element of service provision. Multicultural issues become increasingly important in our multicultural society. Prevention of serious problems is enhanced when mothers receive prenatal and postnatal training in caring for themselves and their children. Several authors have now argued for the use of these kinds of models to treat a variety of family problems including conduct disorder.

Project Ecosystems

Project Ecosystems cannot be properly introduced without first describing its predecessor, Project 12-Ways, an ecobehavioral approach to the treatment and prevention of child abuse and neglect. Project Ecosystems is a systematic replication of Project 12-Ways.

Project 12-Ways was created in 1979 with the premise that problems as serious as child abuse and neglect (CAN) must be multifaceted in etiology and thus in need of a multifaceted approach to assessment and treatment. The ecobehavioral model seemed a natural approach to these serious societal problems.

Child abuse and neglect have only been truly recognized as problems for human services since the mid-1960s when Henry Kempe and his associates published their classic article on the "battered-child syndrome" (Kempe, Silverman, Steele, Droegemueller, & Silver, 1962). Shortly thereafter, the professional world began to develop theories about the etiology of these problems and researchers began to collect mostly demographic data. Early in this process the dominant theory was intrapersonal; that is, child abuse was seen as a problem of the intrapsychic aspects of the perpetrating parent. Gradually, this emphasis began to change and sociological theories gained prominence. In recent times, the prevailing theories have become multidimensional, taking into account the characteristics of the parent and the child, the sociological circumstances of the family, genetics, and what Lutzker (1984) called the family ecosystem.

In 1979 treatment focused primarily on teaching parents alternatives to corporal punishment in disciplining their children or on providing stress reduction to parents in the form of progressive muscle relaxation. Project 12-Ways combined these treatment strategies and added a number of other strategies to address problems in the family ecosystem. These additional strategies included: teaching family activities, training in health and nutrition, using prevention strategies, increasing home safety (Tertinger, Greene, & Lutzker, 1984; Barone, Greene, & Lutzker, 1986), providing counseling and problem-solving strategies, teaching self-control training, providing group support, and teaching money management.

What makes Project 12-Ways ecobehavioral is its focus on multifaceted treatment and particularly that all services are delivered in-home or in situ. Most training takes place, in the families' homes, but some training is also provided in schools, in foster care homes, at preschools, and even in grocery stores and shopping malls. This in-situ approach is successful for two reasons. First, the behavioral principles governing generalization suggest that behavior changed or taught in the setting in which it occurs is more durable. Second, the circumstances (ecosystems) of the families served by Project 12-Ways are such that many are unable or unwilling to go to a clinic or to a university to receive services related to their involvement with the state's child protective services.

The Illinois Department of Children and Family Services is the referral source for Project 12-Ways. Clients are referred because they have been investigated for child abuse or neglect and sufficient evidence of abuse or neglect has been found, or because sufficient evidence exists to suspect child abuse or neglect. Additionally, young single parents are referred if they meet fiscal criteria that qualify them for prevention services, because it is well known that single, poor, young parents are at particular high risk for child abuse and neglect. For CAN families, the only restrictions for services are if the parents are undergoing treatment for drug abuse or the child or parent displays schizophrenia, in which case they are not eligible to receive services from Project 12-Ways.

A Project 12-Ways Case Example

Many children and many parents served by Project 12-Ways have developmental disabilities. This was neither a requirement nor an exclusion for services. Working with parents with developmental disabilities presents particular challenges in providing parent training. Sometimes standardized parent training programs can be modified for parents with developmental disabilities; sometimes new programs based on old, well-worn procedures are needed. For example, Sarber, Halasz, Messmer, Bickett, and Lutzker (1983) treated a family in which the mother suffered from mild mental retardation and illiteracy. Her 4.5-year-old daughter had been removed from the home of this single parent because of what was called nutritional neglect. The mother was unable to plan or shop for nutritious meals. Prior to intervention by Project 12-Ways and the removal of the child, her basic diet consisted of bologna sandwiches, milk, and some packaged foods such as potato chips—for breakfast, lunch, and dinner. The child was never served whole grains or vegetables and fruits.

The first task of Project 12-Ways counselors was to assess whether the mother had any understanding of nutritious meal planning. Given her inability to read, an assessment tool had to be developed. A meal planning board was created. This was a large poster board on which were glued 12 small pocket envelopes in three rows of four columns. At the bottom of the board, under the four rows of envelopes, were four different colored index cards. The envelopes were used for pict. s of foods representing the four basic food groups. The three rows represented breakfast, lunch, and dinner.

Countless photos of foods representing the four basic food groups had been clipped out of magazines and placed on index cards, with duplicates of each food picture. The colors of the cards were the same as those on the planning board. Thus, white cards represented the dairy group, and all pictures of dairy products were placed on white cards. Green represented fruits and vegetables, and those pictures were placed on green cards and so on.

To plan a nutritious meal, the client was asked to place one picture in each pocket. Without training, she did this task randomly, without regard for nutrition. Training consisted of using match-to-sample procedures and social reinforcement. Match-to-sample training involves presenting a sample, a photograph in this case, and asking the client to imitate the sample (model). With the mother in this example, social praise served as the reinforcer for a correct response. In the rare event that this woman failed to match her response to the sample, the counselor simple modeled it for her again, and she then imitated it correctly. This woman thoroughly enjoyed participating in this training. Whenever the counselor appeared for the appointment at her home, the client would ask if they were going to plan meals that day.

The client was taught to match the color of the index card to the index card at the bottom of the planning board. In doing so, each food group was represented in each meal. This simple procedure allowed the client to plan nutritious meals 100 percent of the time. She maintained this skill in formal follow-up assessments after several weeks and months.

The next step in training was to teach this mother to shop for the meals she had planned. Again, a match-to-sample procedure was used. The counselors provided her with a small two-ring binder containing many plastic pocket pages. For each meal she had planned, she looked at the photos from the meal planning board and found another matching picture to put in her binder. Through this process the client was able to make a shopping list by matching the pictures from the planner.

The final stage in training was for the mother to take her binder "shopping list" to the grocery store and use match-to-sample procedures one more time, matching the picture on each page of her binder to foods on the store shelf.

A multiple baseline design represents a single-subject research design that is used to demonstrate that treatment or training, and not some extraneous event, is responsible for behavior change. In this case, training was introduced sequentially across time. This was accomplished by training the client to shop for only one food group at a time. By doing this, we demonstrated that it was the training and not other events in the woman's life that produced the skill. Had other events been responsible for the change, she should have shown shopping skill for all the food groups. The use of a multiple baseline design can also be accomplished across settings or across individuals.

This multiple baseline design across food groups served two purposes. First, it documented that the training procedures were indeed responsible for the changes in her shopping skills. Second, it served a clinical purpose to train across food groups so as to "shape" on these new skills and not overwhelm her. The training was found to be very durable.

During our rather lengthy involvement with this client, she was able to maintain these skills. Also of great interest was that during the training a larger supermarket was built within walking distance of her home. Thus, we had an opportunity to assess generalization of her shopping skills, something she demonstrated 100 percent correctly in the new and larger store.

Over several years, this client received other services from Project 12-Ways. As with other parents with developmental disabilities, we adapted our parent training program in child management skills for her. In this case, we had only modest success. The client became reasonably effective in the use of praise, but her ability to structure activities for her daughter and to provide salient commands was never mastered. Additional services included money management, stress reduction, and some social skills training for the mother.

This case represents a clear example of the ecobehavioral model. Services were delivered in situ and were direct and multifaceted in nature. For most of the time we worked with this woman, she was able to maintain her daughter in the home, and this continued after our services were terminated.

Project Ecosystems: A Systematic Replication

Over the years, through program evaluation, Project 12-Ways has demonstrated its success (Lutzker & Rice, 1987; Lutzker, Wesch, & Rice, 1984; Wesch & Lutzker, 1991). These studies have shown that families who received services from Project 12-Ways were less likely to be recidivistic in CAN than families in the region involved in CAN who did not receive services from Project 12-Ways. Data have also indicated that families referred to Project 12-Ways had more severe problems than the comparison CAN families in that these families had spent more years of involvement with child protective services than had the comparison families (Wesch & Lutzker, 1991).

We were interested in whether the model used in Project 12-Ways could be applied to families with children with developmental disabilities. Thus, Project Ecosystems was begun with a grant from the California Department of Developmental Services. It later became what is known in California as a private vendor service; that is, we contract with state-mandated regional centers to provide our services.

Project Ecosystems is a systematic replication of Project 12-Ways in that the ecobehavioral model is used. However, several aspects differentiate it from Project 12-Ways. First, of course, are the clients. Although many parents and children served by Project 12-Ways had developmental disabilities, that was not a prerequisite for service. Families served by Project Ecosystems, on the other hand, must have a child with developmental disabilities. Project Ecosystems also serves residents of care facilities, and we opened a day services program for adults. The referral criteria for Project Ecosystems are that the child or care resident must have behavioral excesses or deficits of sufficient severity that the client is at risk of placement in a more restrictive setting. Such individuals are also at higher risk for abuse because of their challenging behavior.

The families served by Project 12-Ways live almost exclusively in rural settings. Families served by Project Ecosystems are predominately urban, although rural families are also served, particularly in the desert. Virtually all the families served by Project 12-Ways were poor; most Project Ecosystems families are middle class. Most of Project 12-Ways households were single-parent; most of Project Ecosystems households are two-parent.

All the direct service staff of Project 12-Ways were students or staff members of the Rehabilitation Institute at Southern Illinois University. Direct service providers on Project Ecosystems are graduate and undergraduate students in psychology, social work, and other human service disciplines from a number of southern California universities.

Project Ecosystems and Project 12-Ways are both based on an ecobehavioral model. All services are delivered in-home or in situ. Treatments and assessments are multifaceted, and there is active programming for generalization. Treatment procedures come from the methodology of behavior analysis and therapy, and humanistic counseling and problem solving. Additionally, Project Ecosystems counselors serve as resource specialists for the families that they serve.

The direct service staff of Project Ecosystems are students from local universities. We prefer to utilize students because we believe they are the best service providers for this population. In addition to their salaries, there are other motivators for students. For example, they often receive practicum or internship credits from their programs for their work on Project Ecosystems. Several dissertations and theses have been produced on the project. It is our belief that a research focus to a service project keeps the clinical services "state-of-the-art." An intangible aspect of students as staff is that they are a long way from "burnout." In fact, they are convinced they are "doing good," and they are! Finally, we feel that our devotion to quality control in staff training (see Chapter 9) makes for high quality student-staff who are devoted to serving our clients.

Project Ecosystems Services

Parent/Child Relationship Training

There are two major components to parent/child training. The first is compliance training. In doing this, we often use a modified version of our parent/child training program from Project 12-Ways, a modification of the work of Forehand and McMahon (1981). We prefer their model to other parent training models because of its focus on antecedents and on treatment criteria. That is, before learning to provide consequences, the parent is taught to enrich the environment by attending to the child and to use alpha commands. Alpha commands are simple, discrete commands that can be followed within a few seconds. Alpha commands are especially desirable for use with children with developmental disabilities because these commands increase the likelihood of compliance. Parents usually give far too many beta commands; that is, commands that are too complex, commands given in multiples, and commands in which the parents interrupt compliance.

Another important aspect of compliance training is that criteria are established for the mother to move through training phases. We prefer such a model because it makes treatment decisions less arbitrary. For example, if a mother is only providing one "attend" per minute to her daughter, we might specify a criterion of four per minute before she is taught the next component of training.

Planned activities training (Sanders & Dadds, 1982) comprises the other major component of our parent/child training program. This focuses on affect, structured activities, and incidental teaching. Affect includes tone, command style, talking to children at eye-to-eye level, active and passive touch, and subtle aspects of contingency management. Parents are also taught to plan activities for their children, especially during problem times such as shopping outings and other family trips, at meal preparation time, and after school. Incidental teaching (Hart & Risley, 1975) imbeds teaching into each activity. For example, the activity could be a chore such as setting the table. In showing the child how to do this, the mother would also be instructed to review the child's utensil vocabulary.

Our research (Harrold, Lutzker, Campbell, & Touchette, 1992) has suggested that planned activities training is at least as effective as contingency management training and that parents prefer it to the latter. Furthermore, additional research has suggested that parents generalize their planned activity skills quite well to multiple community settings (Huynen & Lutzker, 1992). It is our belief that planned activities training is more natural for parents to do than contingency management. Consequently, its results may be more durable over time.

Basic Skills Training

Some basic skills are taught directly to children by our counselors and are later taught to parents for maintenance. Other skills are taught to the parents for them to teach to their children. We see a number of children with self-feeding problems. Most frequently, we begin by training self-feeding directly to the child while having the mother observe us using physical prompts, manual guidance, food preference or activity reinforcers, and fading. Also, we fade our teaching into the mother's hands as the child and mother begin to improve their skills. A long list of basic skills have been taught, including toileting, communication, hygiene, safety, and a variety of chores.

Recently, we described a case study in which a child with very serious challenging behaviors was taught functional communication skills, and the challenging behaviors were eliminated (Campbell & Lutzker, 1993). The challenging behaviors were prolonged tantrums (up to several hours) and property destruction. Viewing these problems as communication deficits, the child and his parents were taught signing skills including the ability to express *I want*. Once this training began to reduce the challenging behaviors, the parents were taught planned activities training, especially for community outings, and the challenging behaviors disappeared.

Behavioral Pediatrics

Behavioral pediatrics includes working with parents to help them with compliance to the medical regimens of their children (Lowe & Lutzker, 1979), to allay medical fears, and to treat some problems directly. In compliance, by way of example, we might set up a simple token reinforcement system to help a mother achieve compliance with her child using asthma inhalation medication. An example of fears would be a child with autism who engaged in severe tantrums if he suspected that his mother was taking him to the pediatrician. We successfully remediated this problem in fewer than a dozen treatment sessions by making access to his handheld video game contingent upon his imitating successive steps in the treatment program that were modeled to him by our counselor. The steps began with merely sitting in the car and progressed to sitting in the parking lot at the physician's office, pushing the elevator button, and so on. After this simple program, the child was able to visit the pediatrician whenever necessary.

An example of direct treatment of a medical problem was our work with a boy with severe mental retardation whose seizures were preceded by hyperventilation (Kiesel, Lutzker, & Campbell, 1989). Antecedents to the hyperventilation were demands or excitement. Thus, if the child was asked to clean his room, he might hyperventilate; or if he were told that he was going to an amusement park, he might hyperventilate. Treatment consisted of teaching him behavioral relaxation training (Poppen, 1988) and providing reinforcement for compliance to this treatment regimen. Data were collected at home and at school. A multiple baseline design showed that the behavioral relaxation training was clearly responsible for nearly eliminating hyperventilation-related seizures.

With the frequent medical problems associated with developmental disabilities, behavioral pediatrics is a necessary ingredient in an ecobehavioral approach to working with our families.

Stress Reduction

Stress is a routine element of being a parent. However, parents involved in CAN are less able to deal with the multiple stressors that govern their lives, and the literature has suggested that stress and depression are more apparent in parents (particularly mothers) with children with developmental disabilities (Dyson, 1991). Thus, we include the Beck Depression Inventory (BDI) in our assessments (Beck & Beamesderfer, 1974). If the BDI indicates that the mother is depressed, we suggest counseling for her. We have also found that we are able to favorably affect BDI scores when the major reason for depression is the parent's inability to manage her child's behavior and we have been successful in changing that behavior.

We also use stress reduction procedures with parents when we are concerned that other counseling is indicated. For example, we often find that learning stress reduction procedures helps parents use behavior management procedures more effectively. As any professional who has tried to teach behavior management procedures to parents has learned, parents often find learning these procedures difficult and frustrating. Thus, learning stress reduction procedures can be a very helpful adjunct to parent training procedures. Finally, in both Project 12-Ways and Project Ecosystems, we have found that for many parents stress reduction training is merely a pleasant way to further the good relationship between the counselor and the client. Thus, we sometimes use these procedures simply because they are nice to do.

Two kinds of stress reduction procedures are used. For most parents who are able to benefit from procedures that use imagery, we use progressive muscle relaxation (Jacobson, 1938), whereby the client learns to identify stress in the basic muscle groups and then learns how to relax those muscle groups. For clients who have difficulty with imagery (and this includes the children we serve), we use behavior relaxation training (BRT) (Poppen, 1988). This involves placing the client in the positions of relaxation without going through the more elaborate verbal descriptions. It is an especially handy procedure for children.

By way of example, we used BRT in combination with a number of other procedures to treat a child with ADHD. BRT helped the child learn to tolerate frustrating situations and helped him with some attention skills.

Problem Solving

A common problem parents express to us is, "I love my child, but I can't take the 24-hour attention he needs." This kind of problem is often solved by putting the parents through formal problem-solving sessions. By teaching the parents to create their own problem-solving solutions, such as learning how to approach the Regional Center for respite care for their children, solutions are reached that have a better likelihood of being successful than those forced on a family by a counselor or an agency worker.

All Project Ecosystems staff are trained in counseling and problem-solving strategies. We use a manual (Borck & Fawcett, 1982) and subsequent hands-on training to ensure that all staff have these skills before they work with our families. Trainees take written quizzes and then learn through modeling and role-playing, practicing their skills with supervisors and then with residents of a group home for clients with dual diagnoses (M.R./M.I.) or with participants of one of our day programs. Once they gain proficiency with the group home clients, they then use the procedures with our families.

Using a generalization strategy that Stokes and Baer (1977) referred to as "mediating generalization," parents are able to transfer the problem-solving strategies they have been taught on one problem to new problems without any direct training for those new problems. We remind them of the strategies they were taught and ask them whether they can apply them to the new problem. In most cases, little other training is needed.

We have also used problem-solving strategies with high-functioning older clients. Often these techniques have been used with problems related to inappropriate sexual behavior. In one case, we worked with a young woman in a sheltered workshop who had difficulty discriminating when it was appropriate to touch men in an affectionate way. In addition to some direct contingency management that we taught the workshop managers, we used the problem-solving strategies with this young woman to help her decide alternative ways of showing affection in public and work settings.

The counseling component of the problem-solving package is equally important. We have found that in working with parents, children, and older clients, using humanistic counseling procedures involving active listening and reflective statements goes a long way toward allowing us to intervene with other ecobehavioral procedures.

Assessment

In addition to the specific assessment tools described thus far, all families are provided with a generic assessment. We use the model of functional assessment described by O'Neill, Horner, Albin, Storey, and Sprague (1990). This involves interviews with parents and teachers, record keeping, and direct observations.

A functional assessment is essential for gathering information necessary to design an effective ecobehavioral treatment program. As O'Neill et al. (1990) suggest, there are three elements to an effective functional assessment. The first is interviewing relevant individuals regarding the target child or problem. This may include interviewing the child, the parents, teachers, housekeepers, baby sitters, siblings, grandparents, and anyone else who can provide relevant information that can be used in treatment. Direct observation is the second element of a functional assessment. This involves collecting frequency data through event sampling, time sampling, interval recording, or duration recording. Parents are usually asked to keep frequency data or, occasionally, duration data (such as the duration of a tantrum). When possible, second observers and the counselor collect direct time sampling and interval data, and teachers are frequently asked to collect time sampling data. Further, when a second observer cannot accompany the counselor, videotape is used so a second observer can independently score data from the videotape. Finally, systematic manipulations may occur to provide additional information for the functional assessment.

We will use the fictional Anderson family as an example of how a functional assessment might be accomplished. The problems of the Andersons represent the kinds of problems that each family seen by Project Ecosystems faces, even though the demographics and circumstances of the individual families differ. As will be seen throughout this book, our focus is on treating the ecosystem issues rather than seeing Sean's noncompliance as a singular problem. Interviews would be conducted with the parents and Sean's sister, Adrian. Sean's level of functioning is such that it would be unlikely that a counselor would interview Sean directly. Also, Sean's teachers at the developmental center would be interviewed.

O'Neill and associates (1990) provide a form for interviews. This form asks questions involving descriptions of the challenging behaviors. Included in the descriptions are the topography, frequency, duration, and intensity of the behavior. After obtaining this information, the interviewee is asked about ecological events that could affect behavior, such as medication, medical complications, sleep, eating, and diet routines.

Next, a typical activity schedule is created. This can be very useful in identifying potential ecological events that might explain some problems or that might be rearranged to produce change. For example, in interviewing the Andersons, the counselor determined that Sean was having sleep problems and that two events seemed to affect this: Sean drank about six glasses of caffeinated soda each day; and Sean's father often wrestled with Sean shortly before bedtime. The counselor recommended that caffeine-free soda be substituted for the regular cola. The counselor also recommended that Dave Anderson wrestle with Sean after Dave comes home from work. Before bedtime, a routine was established for Sean. Sean would be given a bath, then he would lie in bed for a story to be read to him, and Dave or Cynthia would stroke Sean's forehead while reading him the story.

Other questions regarding ecology include activities, people who work with the child, staffing patterns, such as those at Sean's developmental center, and what outcomes are monitored. The next section of the functional assessment involves trying to establish possible antecedents for challenging behavior, such as the time of day, the settings, individuals who are frequently present and ongoing activities and situations.

When a particular aide was present at the developmental center, Sean always displayed a tantrum. This allowed the counselor to focus on the aide. The aide paid next to no attention to appropriate behavior and tried to stop Sean's tantrums by hugging him. The problem with this scenario is that the only attention (reinforcement) Sean was receiving was for inappropriate behavior. To correct this, the aide taught to give social attention for appropriate behavior instead of hugging Sean when he acted out. A simple "sit and watch" technique might be used for mild disruptive behavior, whereby Sean would be removed from the group and asked to sit in a chair and watch how the other children get along. This would be done for two or three minutes, then Sean would be asked to join the other children.

The next section of the functional assessment involves "defining the efficiency of the undesirable behavior" (O'Neill et al., 1990, p. 21). This includes an assessment of the physical effort involved in the behavior, the "payoff" for the behavior, and the temporal aspects of the behavior and its consequences. Also of importance in this stage of the functional assessment is learning what other attempts have been made or what other programs have been developed to deal with the challenging behavior of the client. At Project Ecosystems, we often find that other "behavioral" programs have been tried with the family.

Environmental manipulations involve restructuring an aspect of the family ecosystem to determine how it affects behavior. For example, the Andersons might be asked to let Sean ride the bus to the developmental center instead of having his mother drive him. This would allow us to see how he would behave on the bus, how the new routine might affect his behavior in school and at home and, if there were no deleterious effects of him riding the bus, how the family ecosystem might be affected, hopefully for the better, with Cynthia having an hour more per day without Sean because of not having to drive him to and from the developmental center.

At the day programs operated by Project Ecosystems, an environmental manipulation might involve a comparison of how well clients learn social skills when taught by a counselor or a peer (after the peer received training, of course). At school, or in Sean's case at the developmental center, we might examine his on-task behavior across two different seating arrangements.

In addition to the functional assessment described by O'Neill et al. (1990), we also utilize some of the assessment recommendations made by Sanders and Dadds (1993). In particular, these include a developmental history and a mental health assessment of the family members. The mental health history examines affect, motor activity, language, and social responses to the interviewer, when possible, through content and abnormal thoughts and experiences.

Subsequent chapters cover assessments related to the specific service covered by each chapter. It is our strong belief that a good ecobehavioral treatment program is only as good as the assessment.

Summary

Project Ecosystems is a systematic replication of Project 12-Ways. It is an ecobehavioral model in which services are provided in situ, generalization strategies are incorporated in all treatment techniques, and the problems of families with children with developmental disabilities are viewed as multifaceted, in need of multifaceted assessment and services.

CHAPTER FOUR

Parent/Child
Relationship Training

Historically, behavioral parent training has involved teaching parents, usually the mother, basic behavioral procedures such as positive reinforcement, time-out, and shaping. Some training has taken place in homes, although most has taken place in clinics wherein a therapist provides guidance to the parent employing these techniques, usually with the child present.

Behavior management or behavior modification was introduced at the University of Washington preschool laboratories in the mid-1960s. Pioneering work was accomplished with an isolate child (Allen, Hart, Buell, Harris, & Wolf, 1964). Using shaping and social reinforcement procedures, the researchers reversed the contingencies that were maintaining the child's isolate behavior. Prior to treatment, whenever the child was not involved in interactions with other children the teachers spent considerable time and attention consoling her and asking her why she chose not to participate with other children. This inadvertently provided reinforcement for the iso-late behavior. The treatment involved having the teachers ignore the child when she was isolate and providing attention and praise for approxima-tions by the child of joining the other children. This process is known as shaping. This differential reinforcement of other behavior (DRO procedure) was highly effective in reversing the child's nonsocial behavior, and so the field of behavior modification was born.

At approximately the same time, several of the researchers at the Uni-versity of Washington were asked to become involved in the treatment of a child with autism and other complications, such as aggression, tantrums, and self-injurious behavior. Until this time, little or no success had been re-ported in working with children with autism. These unfortunate children were doomed to a life of self-stimulation, sometimes self-injury, persever-ation, and behavior that was far behind developmental norms. Children with autism remained in their self-stimulation worlds and seldom interacted with others. Based on the success of these revolutionary behavior modifi-cation techniques, the behavioral researchers were asked to deal with Dickey, a 3.5-year-old boy with autism (Wolf, Risley, & Mees, 1964). Dickey displayed severe self-injury, had few self-help or language skills, no social skills, and all of this was complicated by the fact that Dickey had cataracts on his eyes that required surgery. Dickey would go blind if the cataracts were not surgically removed, and he would go blind if they were removed and he did not subsequently wear his glasses. In anticipation of the sur-gery, professionals had tried to get Dickey to wear "practice" glasses, but he would violently remove them even when the glasses were strapped around his head. Thus, teaching Dickey to wear glasses became an impor-tant treatment priority.

A number of behavior modification techniques based on animal labo-ratory precedents using operant conditioning techniques were employed with Dickey. Extinction (that is, removing reinforcement) was used in a specially designed room to eliminate his self-injurious behavior (SIB). The researchers had guessed correctly that this behavior was being maintained by attention. Thus, when attention (reinforcement) was removed, the SIB disappeared. In the meantime, social praise was being paired with bits of breakfast and sweetened cereal for correct simple language responses in training using modeling, imitation, and reinforcement. Finally, a shaping program was begun wherein Dickey was given social and edible reinforce-ment for making successive physical approximations toward his glasses, which were sitting on a table. Ultimately, these shaping procedures were used to get him to pick up the glasses and finally to wear them for increas-ing periods of time.

The results of this intense work were dramatic. Dickey had successful surgery and readily wore his glasses. His self-injurious behavior was elimi-nated, and he developed language and social skills. By the time he was

14 years old, Dickey was developmentally normal (Nedelman & Sulzbacher, 1972).

Following these early successes at the University of Washington, researchers elsewhere began to explore the use of behavior management techniques in a variety of areas, particularly with parents as the mediators of change. Thus, the field of behavioral parent training began to develop by the late 1960s. Some parents were taught by behavior therapists directly in their homes; however, most were taught in clinics or laboratory (analog) settings. Treatment usually consisted of teaching the parents to use simple procedures such as social and primary (food and drink) reinforcement, extinction, time-out (brief isolation), shaping, and in the 1970s, overcorrection. Overcorrection involves having the child repeatedly practice the desired behavior after having failed to do so. For example, when a child wets his pants, he would be asked to show the correct steps in going to the bathroom for ten consecutive trials.

Simple token reinforcement programs were also taught to parents. Token reinforcement involves establishing the value of points, stickers, or plastic chips as generalized reinforcers similar to money in everyday life. Through gradual training, a child is taught that tokens, points, or stickers have "backups," such as food, drink, or privileges. To teach this to a child with mental retardation, the teacher or therapist might start by giving the child a plastic chip immediately contingent upon a correct response, such as imitating a verbal model. The chip is immediately traded for a sip of apple juice. Gradually, a delay is built in between delivery of the chip and the trade-in. Also gradually, the number of chips required for a trade-in is increased as is the number of items used as backups.

These procedures were applied to problems such as noncompliance, bedwetting, language delays, self-injury and self-stimulation, hearing deficits, chronic medical problems, child abuse and neglect, conduct disorders, and feeding disorders. Methods of teaching parents have included lecture, bibliotherapy, modeling, role-playing, and the use of video techniques (Lutzker & Martin, 1981). Various durations of filmed modeling techniques were also examined.

The success of behavior modification in the 1960s and early 1970s was exciting. A whole new technology was born, and those who supported a scientific base for psychological treatment were pleased with the empirical approaches offered by behavior modification. The empiricism was evident in the manner in which behavior modification was conducted. Assessment and treatment were based on direct observation of behavior rather than on reliance on psychometric tools. Treatment was based on principles derived from laboratory research rather than on untestable concepts; and data were gathered from direct observations that allowed simple single-subject research designs to document the relationship between the intervention techniques and the behavior change.

Of course, there were critics outside this new field, and criticism appeared later within the field as well. Early critics expressed concern that behavior modification techniques were cold and not humanistic, that the focus was on narrow aspects of the parent/child relationship, such as compliance, and that these procedures could actually be harmful to children because the children would respond like trained animals (Gordon, 1975).

Concerns within the field began to appear in the mid-1970s. Bothered by the use of behavior management procedures in the classroom, Winett and Winkler (1972) argued that behavioral psychologists were shaping a generation of children to "be still, be quiet, be docile." Other behavioral researchers were concerned that the very empiricism on which the field so prided itself was showing some flaws in outcome in behavioral parent training. For example, in a comprehensive study, Bernal, Klinnert, and Schultz (1980) compared behavioral parent training to client-centered training for families with behavior problem children. Trained observers corroborated parents' ratings, finding that parents who received child behavior therapy rated it higher than did parents who received client-centered therapy. However, follow-up data from the observers indicated an equal decline in treatment gains in both groups, even though parents who received child behavior therapy believed the outcome had remained favorable. Thus, the Bernal et al. (1980) data suggest that child behavior therapy may not be as durable over time as would be desired.

Sallis (1983) expressed concern that little research in parent training explored generalization or how to produce it. Lutzker, McGimsey, McRae, and Campbell (1983) also expressed concern that child behavior therapy had not been responsive to its critics and that it in fact focused on a narrow range of family concerns. They asserted that, despite its empirical roots, more often that not, behavioral parent training lacked data on the independent variable. That is, although reliable data were always presented, data were lacking on how treatment was delivered. For example, if a parent is the mediator of behavior change procedures, observers should collect data not only on child outcome but also on the frequency or rate at which the parents deliver the procedures they were trained to deliver. Lutzker and associates were also concerned that treatment described in research articles is most often delivered by graduate students and not by experienced therapists; therefore, the database in child behavior therapy comes from other than what might actually occur in the broader professional community.

It has been argued that time-out techniques may be the critical element in parent training (Forehand, 1986). However, Lutzker, Touchette, and Campbell (1988) believe that time-out may be the least relevant component of child behavior therapy and that the emphasis should be placed on the family as an ecosystem. For example, Singer, Irvine, and Irvin (1989) have suggested that parent training for families with children with developmental disabilities should involve compliance training, social support, marital discord counseling, and teaching parents how to deal with schools and agencies. These authors advocate many components of the ecobehavioral approach presented here.

The 1980s and 1990s have shifted the focus from a narrow view of parent training for parents with children with developmental disabilities to the recognition that a family needs access to a variety of resources: coping skills (Summers, Behr, & Turnbull, 1989), support services (Warren & Warren, 1989), an understanding of their values (Taylor, Knoll, Lehr, & Walker, 1989), and school support (Halvorsen, Doering, Farron-Davis, Usilton, & Sailor, 1989). With this expanded viewpoint, compliance training using reinforcement and time-out becomes a small aspect of a more comprehensive approach to treating the family.

Planned Activities Training

One of the limitations of reinforcement and time-out training approaches to parent training with parents of children with developmental disabilities is that these procedures may be effective only when the home environment is enriched. In a critically important study, Solnick, Rincover, and Peterson (1977) found that access to time-out acted as a reinforcer when the teaching environment was "impoverished" and that time-out was effective only when the child was removed from a very stimulating teaching situation. More recently, Haring and Kennedy (1990) found that time-out was not effective in a demand teaching situation. It was effective only when students were in situations that Haring and Kennedy labeled *leisure*. Demand situations, such as academic work in school and commands from parents at home commonly cause noncompliance and even SIB in children with developmental disabilities. Thus, time-out has several constraints. In particular, it may be ineffective in the many demand situations confronting the client.

If consequences such as time-out pose practical, ethical, and outcome concerns, a focus on antecedents to facilitate traditional compliance training would seem especially prudent. By antecedents, we mean stimulus events that precede behavior by setting the occasion for it to occur. For example, in everyday life, one of the most salient antecedents is a traffic light; it sets the occasion for stopping or going in a car. For clients of our services, antecedents can set the occasion for appropriate behavior, such as responding correctly to a model showing a self-help skill, or set the occasion for challenging behavior. We served a family that complained that whenever the mother told her adult son that he was going to work, he engaged in a tantrum. Because he otherwise appeared to enjoy work, we saw the mother's telling him that it was time to go to work as a potential or probable antecedent for the challenging behavior. Thus, in this simple (and probably lucky!) example, our "treatment" was to ask the mother to simply wake her son, tell him to get dressed, but not mention work. In this case, elimination of the antecedent of telling him he was going to work was sufficient to eliminate the tantrums.

Another focus using antecedents is planned activities training (PAT), which has been shown to facilitate contingency management training (Sanders & Dadds, 1982) and even replace it (Huynen & Lutzker, 1992). PAT involves teaching parents to organize and plan activities with their children. Further, it teaches parents to use incidental teaching techniques (Hart & Risley, 1975), which adds an educational focus to the parent training. Incidental teaching means that the parent is taught to provide verbal and physical instruction related to whatever activity is going on between the parent and the child. For example, the mother and the child might be grocery shopping. The parent would be taught to ask the child which box of detergent was larger, which one has red on the box, or, if the child can recognize letters, which box has a big "T" on it.

In addition to incidental teaching, parents are taught to focus on good behavior and to self-evaluate their own performance and their use of the PAT strategies. Traditional contingency management (child behavior modification) is subtly built into the PAT techniques. Parents are taught to praise appropriate behavior and to ignore minor misbehavior, but this training is far less formal and detailed than that used to teach traditional contingency management techniques. There is usually little need to teach techniques for behavior reduction, because challenging behavior frequently ceases to occur, undoubtedly because parents learn to actively engage their children in activities that prevent misbehavior.

We have found that parents generalize PAT to activities within and outside the home. We have observed them using these techniques in the car, at grocery stores, at shopping malls, at relatives' homes, and even at churches and synagogues. Also, many parents report spontaneously using PAT with their other children. Parents have expressed a preference for PAT as opposed to more structured contingency management techniques (Harrold, Lutzker, Campbell, & Touchette, 1992).

We saw a family in which the mother was unable to take her 6-year-old child with autism anywhere in public, especially to the grocery store. After five sessions of PAT, the mother had generalized the skills she had learned at home very well and was applying them to a number of community settings. So well had she and her child learned the procedures that when they arrived at the grocery store the *child* said to the mother, "Now, mom, are we going to go over the rules for being in the store?"

We use PAT with almost every family, in addition to whatever other services we might provide. Table 4.1 provides an outline of the way PAT progresses through multiple sessions with a client. The diagnosis of the child is relevant only in choosing the kinds of activities we might recommend to the parents and the level of teaching required. We have found PAT to be effective with children with all levels of mental retardation and with children with other diagnoses, such as autism, Fragile X syndrome, and ADHD.

Table 4.1 *Planned Activities Training Sessions*

Session I
a. negotiate an agenda
b. review progress
c. identify problem settings
d. provide rationale for PAT
e. preparation, time management, and organization
f. how to discuss rules with children in noncoercive manner
g. selecting activities for home and community settings
h. incidental teaching
i. natural and tangible positive reinforcers
j. practical consequences
k. post-activity discussions with children
l. summary

Session II
a. review agenda
b. review homework
c. model procedural checklists
d. model community setting checklist
e. establish goals
f. summary

Session III
a. review agenda
b. practice encouraging independent play when parent is busy
c. practice incidental teaching and structured play
d. feedback
e. establish goals

Session IV
a. review agenda
b. practice independent play training
c. practice getting ready to go out
d. feedback
e. goals

Session V
a. review agenda
b. review progress
c. practice PAT with minimal assistance
d. self-evaluation
e. problem solving for the future
f. goals
g. model checklist for community setting

Source: Adapted from M. R. Sanders and M. R. Dadds, *Planned Activities Training* (Brisbane: University of Queensland Press, 1987).

By way of example, we treated a family with a 3-year-old boy with autism. The child had yet to develop speech, displayed frequent tantrums (especially when demands were placed on him), was almost 100 percent noncompliant to parental commands, and had sleep problems. We dealt with the sleep problems by conducting a behavioral assessment. This brought to our attention that the child was given more than a gallon of chocolate milk per day because it was one of the few foods he liked. We also determined that he spent very little time in structured activities and that he had no bedtime routine.

First, we had the mother switch from chocolate milk to carob milk, thus eliminating the caffeine he was consuming from the chocolate. He drank the carob milk as readily as he drank the chocolate milk. We also had her develop a bedtime routine that involved apprising the boy 15 minutes before bedtime that bedtime was going to begin in 15 minutes. We instructed her to help him get ready for bed, to read two stories to him, and to stroke his head when she read the stories. It is possible that these changes alone were responsible for him sleeping through the night and not leaving his bed when he was put to sleep, but we also increased the number of activities the parent and the child engaged in throughout the day through PAT (PAT was also used to establish the bedtime routine). The child was probably better able to sleep because he was more active during the day. The PAT took only five sessions with this mother, which is the usual number of sessions required.

Another example of the use of PAT was with the depressed single mother of a 5-year-old girl with autism. The mother had considerable difficulty taking the little girl anywhere in public. In a case such as this, we would normally consider stress reduction training for the mother. However, she was receiving ongoing treatment from mental health professionals for her depression, so the treatment of choice for Project Ecosystems was PAT. With only five sessions of PAT, the child showed nearly no misbehavior in shopping situations in which she was almost totally noncompliant previously and would display tantrums. Prior to PAT, the mother engaged in virtually no social/educational interactions with her little girl. After PAT, videotapes revealed nearly constant incidental teaching by the mother during shopping trips.

Greg was a 5-year-old boy with autism. His younger brother had some medical problems that caused frequent vomiting. The mother was at her wit's end trying to manage both children. From the time Greg got home from his special day program at 3 P.M. until he went to sleep after 7 P.M., he was in constant motion. The mother was literally exhausted. She was also unable to take Greg out in public.

PAT involved teaching the parent and child to play with his collection of "little people/toys" in his room. Considerable focus was placed on teaching the mother our incidental teaching techniques. Also, she was taught to structure activities at home and to plan for public outings. Our generalization observations took place in a video store, a grocery store, and during the family's dinners. The mother showed outstanding generalization of her PAT skills, and the child's behavior improved remarkably. The family now has little difficulty going anywhere in public, and the mother no longer feels exhausted.

A final example of PAT is Mark, a 6-year-old boy with ADHD. He had been treated fairly unsuccessfully with medication alone. We taught his mother PAT during several play activities at home. She showed outstanding generalization of these skills as we observed her in the library, the grocery store, a park, and even during Mark's visits to the dentist's office. What the mother learned particularly well that clearly enhanced the results with Mark was to explain each activity in advance and to explain the rules or parameters of behavior on outings. Of course, she then practiced incidental teaching during all these outings and provided social and backup reinforcers for good behavior by Mark.

Affective Skills

Learning to conduct behavior management and activities with children are very important skills for parents; however, another component should be considered as well, namely, affect. In supervising graduate and undergraduate students over many years, we noticed that although most of them mastered behavior management principles, as did many parents, some staff members still lacked rapport with children. We also noted that some parents were less facile with children than were other parents. Thus, we conducted research to determine what good adult/child interaction skills are and whether we could teach them to staff and parents (Lutzker, Megson, Webb, & Dachman, 1985).

To validate what good affect skills are, we sent a questionnaire to child behavior therapists, preschool teachers, and early childhood educators. The questions we asked regarding good adult/child interaction skills were derived from an examination of the early childhood literature, which noted behaviors such as talking to a child at eye level as important. Of the behaviors about which we asked, 13 were rated sufficiently high for us to consider them as important to teach. These behaviors are listed in Table 4.2.

After deciding to teach these 13 skills, we filmed preschool teachers interacting with children. We used the videotapes of these teacher/child interactions for two purposes. One purpose was to determine what training

Table 4.2 *Affective Skills for Adults Interacting with Children*

1. Make clear, precise verbal statements to the child.
2. Show congruence between verbal and physical messages.
3. Have a smiling pleasant facial expressions when interacting with a positively behaving child.
4. Assume an equal position of height with the child.
5. When issuing a command, specify how to comply.
6. Interact primarily with children who are behaving appropriately.
7. Ignore minor disruptive behavior.
8. Avoid scolding.
9. Allow children to engage in passive physical contact with you.
10. Use assertive tone for statements of disapproval.
11. Use assertive tone for statements of approval.
12. Actively initiate physical contact with children.

criteria we would use. That is, we wanted to know how many of these behaviors good preschool teachers displayed. From this information we determined the criteria by which we would train parents and staff. The second reason for videotaping the teachers was to have tapes showing good interactions for use during staff and parent training.

First we collected direct observation measures of staff and parent adult/child interactions. With staff, we did this at a preschool. With parents, we did this in their own homes with their own children. Each staff member and each parent displayed some of the 13 criterion behaviors, but no staff member or parent displayed more than nine of these criterion behaviors. Next, we showed them the definitions of all the behaviors, pointed out the ones on which they were deficient, and praised the criterion behaviors they had displayed. For the behaviors that were not at the desired level of performance, we showed the videotapes of the teachers and asked the staff member or the parent to pay particular attention to those behaviors.

After only one to five training sessions, staff and parents demonstrated all criterion behaviors. Further, staff showed generalization of their performance to children with whom they had not previously interacted, and parents showed generalization to children in their family with whom we had not trained the parent to use these skills.

Planned activities training and contingency management training reflect what we call *effective* behavior management. This adult/child interaction training reflects *affective* behavior management. Parents have also reported that they feel more positive toward their children after receiving this "affect" training.

Contingency Management

In addition to PAT and affect training, we also employ more traditional contingency management programs in the forms of token economies and differential reinforcement of other behaviors (DRO). Token economies involve teaching parents to teach their children point systems. The points are delivered contingent upon the child performing desired target behaviors, such as correct toilet skills, or for compliance and chores around the home. A fixed rule on Project Ecosystems is that our staff are told to ensure success. Point systems (usually charts with happy face stickers) are used to reinforce behavior and are not used as response cost systems whereby points are removed for inappropriate behavior. The father of a young adult living in a group home provided Project Ecosystems counselors and the group home managers with money to "back up" the point system. The money-based token economy produced changes in personal hygiene and compliance by this young adult that the group home managers had been trying to achieve for years.

Shaping principles are used to create these point systems. We usually begin with only one behavior on the chart. When the child is performing that behavior at a criterion level, we add another behavior to the chart. A common mistake made by parents and professionals is introducing too many behaviors at one time.

The traditional contingency management program to which we most closely adhere is the one described by Forehand and McMahon (1981). This involves teaching parents to attend more frequently to their children, to praise more often, how to use simple discreet commands, how to reinforce compliance, and how to use time-out. Of particular note, this model relies on criteria for moving between treatment phases. For example, a mother is not taught how to give commands until she has demonstrated a preset criterion for increasing how often she attends to her child. Similarly, she is not taught reinforcement until she has mastered commands, and so forth. This program adds empirical criteria for performance in a more specific manner than do most other contingency management programs.

Forehand and McMahon (1981) recommend teaching parents to distinguish between alpha commands, which are desirable to use with children and others, and beta commands, which are undesirable, and then teaching them to use only alpha commands with their children. An alpha command is simple and discrete, and compliance should begin to occur within ten seconds. Also, an independent observer must be able to determine what compliance is by the nature of the command. Examples of alpha commands are, "Sean, please pick up those toys from your floor and place them in your toy box," or "Sean, stop hitting your sister, now."

Beta commands come in three varieties. The first is complex; an example of this type of beta command is, "Sean, clean up your room." Although this command may sound simple, it is not specific enough. Does "clean up your room" mean pick up the toys and make your bed? It could mean to tidy your desk, and so on.

The second kind of beta command entails multiple commands, which may have alpha and beta components. For example, Cynthia Anderson might say, "Sean, pick up your toys and place them in your toy box" (an alpha command so far), but in the same breath go on to say, "and take care of your dog" (an unspecific beta command) and "and leave Adrian alone" (also unspecific). When multiple commands are given, the child (and a counselor or observer who may be present) does not know which command to comply with and is less likely to comply at all.

The third kind of beta command may begin as an alpha command, "Sean tie your shoe," but become a beta command if the parent interrupts compliance. Cynthia might lack patience as Sean begins to methodically tie his shoe, and say, "Never mind, I'll do it," thus completing the response for him.

With practice, parents are able to fairly readily distinguish between alpha and beta commands and can learn to use alpha commands almost exclusively.

We have asked our staff to use natural and creative activity reinforcers as backups for the points or stickers on the charts. These are preferable to edible reinforcers. Backup reinforcers include special trips to favorite fast food restaurants; additional games with parents, siblings, or our counselors; trips to malls for small favors; and bus rides.

Shaping must also be used in the introduction of backup reinforcers. In the beginning stages of a token economy, the backups must be available immediately, so they must be simpler than trips to the mall. Once the child associates the points with the backup reinforcers, the reinforcers can be delivered in a more temporally distant manner. With children with developmental disabilities, point systems should not be too complicated. It is important that backup reinforcers be easy to earn, thus enriching the child's environment and limiting any opportunity to fail.

DRO, differential reinforcement of other behavior, has existed since the beginning of behavior modification. Its use seems relevant mostly in conjunction with other more structured programs and with younger children. DRO involves providing reinforcement, usually praise, for any behavior other than some targeted challenging behavior, which is usually ignored. The two primary problems with DRO are that providing reinforcement for any behavior does not ensure that the parent or teacher is otherwise engaged with the child, which we feel is critical, and that ignoring challenging behavior is not an easy thing for many parents and teachers to do. Thus, the procedure lacks some practicality. We always use DRO, but we use it in combination with PAT or other engagement and skill-building activities. Also, when we use DRO, it is with challenging behaviors that are easy for the parent or teacher to ignore, such as simple whining or some kind of innocuous attention-getting behavior.

Resource Specialists

We have found in our many years of providing service to CAN families, to families with children with developmental disabilities, to low SES families, to rural and urban families, and to middle-class families, that we are often surprised at their need for information about services or at their lack of awareness of some critical developmental variables related to their children. Thus, we often see ourselves as resource specialists who provide information or suggest a service to augment our services.

For example, we treated a 4.5-year-old boy with ADHD. His mother was a single parent and a pediatrician who wanted him to excel in school as she had done. We asked about her daily routine, especially bedtime, something we ask all families we treat. We are always concerned that there be some kind of established bedtime routine in each family, and we usually insist that story reading by parents of young children be a part of that routine. Rather than reading stories to her son, this mother was having him read third-grade reading primers to her. We explained to her the need to have a relaxing interaction at bedtime. If she wanted him to read primers to her at another time, that was okay; however, we asked that at bedtime she read to her son. She requested a list of stories, which we provided after consulting with an early childhood specialist. The mother readily complied, and reported that she and her son not only enjoyed the new bedtime routine but that bedtime noncompliance ceased to be a problem.

We have made special reading materials available to parents who wish to learn more about their children's disorders, such as Down syndrome and autism. Depending on the parent's intellectual level, different levels of reading can augment treatment because the parent becomes more aware of the child's potential and limitations. We have found that having parents read many of our response definitions, such as the ones in Table 4.2 regarding affect, go a long way toward facilitating the subsequent "hands-on" training we provide.

It is our opinion that parent training has been too narrowly focused in the past. To produce long-term parental interest, it is necessary to look at the entire family picture in parent training and incorporate the many components we have described here into each individually tailored parent training program. Also, as Wahler and Fox (1980) have advised, we must take into account the contextual variables of the day when we visit a family for parent training. It is important for each counselor to use counseling skills to determine how the mother is feeling on any visit and to have her talk about the entire family situation. If she has had an argument with her husband in the morning, it may not be prudent to do parent training at all on that particular day's visit. Having this kind of training and learning this kind of sensitivity goes a long way toward providing optimal services, such as parent training that has a probability of maintenance of treatment effects.

The issue of setting events in context is going to dominate much research and related service in the decades ahead. We must learn more about how temporally distant setting events affect the current behavior of parents and their children. It is our belief that the ecobehavioral model takes these issues into account much more than narrow behavior management programs have done. Programming for generalization across time, settings, and responses seems to be an inherent aspect of the ecobehavioral model. That we work entirely in situ, that we give parents self-management and problem-solving skills through PAT, and that we assess and treat in a variety of settings dealing with a variety of behaviors seems to produce natural generalization. Thus, we do not rely on what Stokes and Baer (1977) described as a "train and hope" model for producing generalization.

Summary

Early behavior modification efforts produced dramatic positive results for children with autism and mental retardation, but training for parents in these skills was rather narrowly focused. More recently, broader strategies, such as the ecobehavioral model described here, have been useful in teaching parents to manage their children's behavior. In this chapter, we have described planned activities training, contingency management, command training, and teaching parents affective skills with their children. We believe that service providers must take family ecological variables into account when providing services and that issues of context will become an increasingly important component when providing these services.

CHAPTER FIVE

Stress Reduction

Unless they are unusually naive, most parents expect that the arrival of their first child will add stress to the household and the marriage. The new baby will bring financial concerns that may not have been addressed previously. Sleep patterns of the parents will be seriously disturbed for a while. Work and leisure schedules will change for many years. Yet, despite these added stressors, most parents adjust and so do their children. And the parents look forward to watching the development of their children.

For the parents of a child with developmental disabilities, all the normal stressors apply; however, a host of additional ones also appear and may not dissipate. Not only does the new child disrupt family routine but disappointments mount for the parents as the child fails to meet developmental norms. The parents may feel guilt or uncertainty about the role their habits or genes may have played in the child's developmental delays. The parents may feel abandoned and angry at friends and family who may be judgmental or may see less of the couple because the friends or family are uncomfortable being around the child with developmental disabilities. Or, the child may have serious behavioral excesses or deficits that create difficult problems in social situations.

Going to the grocery store can be a challenge for the parents of any 2 year old, but the parents expect this to change as the child matures. Going to the grocery store or to the mall presents a serious problem for the parents of an 8-year-old child with autism, for the child may try to run away, may have a tantrum, or merely look odd enough to draw stares from adults and audible comments from other children to their parents. So, it should not come as much of a surprise that mothers of children with developmental disabilities must handle more stress and are more depressed than mothers of children without developmental disabilities (Beckman, 1991).

Krauss (1993) has examined the differences and similarities between mothers and fathers of children with disabilities in child-related parenting stress. Fathers reported more stress related to their children's temperaments; mothers reported stress related to the personal consequences of parenting. The implications of this research add further to the argument for an ecobehavioral approach. Krauss (1993) notes that recognizing the need to deal with family stress related to having a child with disabilities demands that attention be paid to the family beyond the treatment for the child with disabilities. This includes a need for stress reduction, early intervention, and family support systems.

We have established that parents of children with developmental disabilities suffer additional stress. Consider the fact that learning new skills may add to this stress. Parents seeking help because of the severe behavioral excesses or deficits of their children are probably unaware that learning new behavior management skills can also be stress producing. Many professionals who teach new contingency management skills to parents teach them to ignore inappropriate behaviors. This skill takes time to master and requires considerable patience on the parents' part, especially considering that the behavior the parents are now trying to ignore has probably been a considerable source of frustration to them. Stress reduction training is an important adjunct for parents of children with developmental disabilities and should be conducted along with any program of behavior management.

Case Studies

Consider the case of a family who was self-referred for prevention of child abuse (Campbell, O'Brien, Bickett, & Lutzker, 1983). This family was referred to Project 12-Ways after the mother called the state's child protective service with a sincere concern that she might kill her 4-year-old daughter if she did not receive some help in managing the child's behavior. The girl was hyperactive and noncompliant and suffered from probable learning disabilities.

Although structured parent training was clearly needed, it had also been determined that the mother suffered from severe disabling migraine headaches for which a neurologist could find no obvious organic etiology. The ecobehavioral perspective of Project 12-Ways dictated that this problem take priority over parent training, because we could not imagine a scenario whereby the mother would be able to do a good job learning command training, providing additional attention, providing contingent praise, and applying time-out while burdened by severe headaches. We provided in-home treatment for her headaches by teaching her deep muscle relaxation and by teaching her to recognize the situations that brought on the stress that led to the headaches. After several weeks of treatment, the average number of weekly headaches was reduced from 14 to one; the average number of minutes of headaches per week declined from 1400 to ten. Only when we began to see evidence that this mother was gaining control of her headaches did we begin parent training. The stress reduction program was designed to reduce the tension headaches and to prevent their onset. Training consisted of utilizing progressive muscle relaxation procedures (Jacobson, 1938) and providing verbal feedback from a behavioral postural checklist (Schilling & Poppen, 1983; Poppen, 1988), which assesses relaxation positions. The mother's level of relaxation was assessed prior to each training session and assessed again after training using the postural checklist.

The training sessions took place in the mother's living room with the mother sitting in a reclining chair. The therapist sat in front of the mother so the ten components of the behavioral postural checklist could be observed and recorded. During the mother's progressive muscle relaxation training sessions, the therapist initially provided the child with toys and activities to distract her from interrupting her mother. After the mother demonstrated the ability to relax, the games and activities were discontinued. This enabled the mother to practice relaxation while experiencing the child's interruptions. Eventually, the mother was able to ignore the interruptions and practice the relaxation.

The behavioral postural checklist included ten behavioral positions. Observations of these behavioral positions were recorded every minute. During the first 30 seconds of each minute, the therapist counted the number of breaths the mother took. This established the baseline rate for breathing. During the next 30 seconds, the therapist documented the occurrence or nonoccurrence of the remaining relaxation positions. To assess the effectiveness of the progressive muscle relaxation procedures on the mother's headaches, she was required to record the frequency, duration, and intensity on a one to ten scale, (one indicating light headache pain; five indicating dull, steady headache pain; eight indicating heavy, throbbing headache pain; and ten indicating incapacitating headache pain). The mother posted her data on the refrigerator to cue herself to record her headaches. She recorded these data regularly and reliably throughout the study. She was also instructed to practice the progressive muscle relaxation exercises at home in the reclining chair in the living room. Once the mother achieved a state of relaxation, she was told to self-monitor her levels of tension twice daily (this self-monitoring occurred between 10:00 A.M. and 12:00 P.M. and again between 2:00 P.M. and 4:00 P.M.). If she was feeling some tension, she was asked to be sure to begin her relaxation exercises.

The stress reduction intervention alleviated the headaches that once incapacitated the mother. The results clearly indicated that once the mother maintained a high level of home practice of the relaxation exercises the frequency and duration of her headaches dropped significantly. This demonstrates a negative correlation between home practice and duration of headaches. Providing the training within the mother's own stress-producing environment (home) quite possibly facilitated the long-term maintenance that was achieved. Now that the mother was considerably more relaxed, she learned the child behavior management procedures rapidly and well and gained remarkable new control over the child's behavior.

During the assessment phase with this family, it was also determined that the marriage was not especially happy or productive. This was formally assessed by the session-by-session administration of the Marital Happiness Scale (Azrin, Naster, & Jones, 1973). Once we were successful with the headache treatment and parent training, we provided in-home reciprocity counseling (Azrin et al., 1973). As a result of this process, the husband acquiesced to the wife's longstanding wish to return to her nursing career. This, along with having the couple work on reciprocity of reinforcement, reduced other stressors in the family environment, especially financial ones. It also meant that the child was able, for the first time, to spend considerable time outside the home in daycare, further reducing the mother's parenting burden. The final marital assessments showed a marriage that was regularly scored as happy. The mother received relief from her headaches and help in her behavior management strategies, and the couple learned to provide mutual reinforcement to each other.

Another example of the use of stress reduction techniques was with a mother served by Project Ecosystems. She had twin daughters, age 4, one of whom had autism. Living next door to this single mother was her own mother who spoke little English. Although our client was very enthusiastic about learning planned activities training for her children, it was apparent that the burden of taking care of these children, trying to acculturate her mother, and trying to survive as a single parent caused her considerable anxiety. During assessment, all clients served by Project Ecosystems are provided with written descriptions of the services to be provided, and the counselor reviews these with the family. After a few PAT sessions, the mother asked for further explication of the stress reduction procedures, and we provided behavior relaxation training (BRT) (Schilling & Poppen, 1983).

BRT involves teaching the client the following postures:

a. slow, deep, regular breathing
b. quiet—no sounds can be heard
c. no noticeable body movement
d. head supported and in the middle of the body
e. eyes closed so that eyelids are smooth
f. lips parted slightly at center
g. no noticeable movement in the neck
h. shoulders rounded and both at the same comfortable height
i. hands in clawlike posture
j. feet pointed away from each other at a comfortable angle

After several sessions, the mother could become profoundly relaxed, and she was asked to practice BRT daily. Once she was practicing daily, she was taught to identify the home situations that caused her to feel tension. Whenever she felt this tension, she was to assume as many BRT postures as she could at the moment. She reported that using these procedures enabled her to implement PAT with good results and to deal more effectively with her own mother.

BRT was used quite successfully to reduce hyperventilation and seizures for a child with profound mental retardation and epilepsy (Kiesel, Lutzker, & Campbell, 1989). Tim, a 6-year-old boy, was referred to Project Ecosystems by a pediatric neurologist. It was the impression of the neurologist and of Tim's mother that most seizures were preceded by hyperventilation. We collected baseline data in school and at home. Once the functional assessment was completed, it was determined that hyperventilation was the antecedent to most seizures. Furthermore, the antecedent to hyperventilation was a demand or a major change in Tim's stimulus situation. An example of the behavioral chain would be: the teacher tells Tim it is time to stop playing with a toy car and time to begin a picture card recognition task, Tim begins to hyperventilate, and then he has a seizure. At home this sequence might even be precipitated by a positive remark from his mother such as announcing that the family would be going to an amusement park.

If we could teach Tim an alternative to hyperventilating, we thought this might preclude most seizure activity. BRT seemed an especially relevant alternative because relaxation is clearly incompatible with hyperventilation. Using modeling, imitation, and social and token reinforcement, we taught BRT to Tim, and subsequently to his mother and his teacher. A multiple baseline design was used. First, the mother implemented BRT at home, and later the teacher did so at school. Both the mother and the teacher were taught to give Tim the cue to relax whenever they were going to place a demand on him or announce a change in the stimulus situation. This training resulted in a dramatic reduction in the frequency of seizures at home and at school.

A recent divorcee with two children under the age of 5 years was having difficulty with her 5-year-old son with Down syndrome. He did not follow directions and had aggressive outbursts. During the initial home assessment, it became apparent that the mother was overcommitted to catering to her son's desires. The mother's daily round of activities included driving one boy to preschool, driving the other boy to a special education setting, then going to work, returning to the special education setting during lunch hour to do volunteer work in the classroom, going back to work, picking up her 5-year-old son, picking up her preschool son, going to physical and speech therapy for her 5-year-old son, coming home to prepare dinner, bathing the boys, working with her special education son, reading to her preschool son, putting them both to bed, and then cleaning the house and washing their clothes. The 5-year-old child regularly attacked his younger brother, destroyed toys, and would not follow directions.

A scatterplot analysis was conducted to pinpoint problem times. A scatterplot (Touchette, McDonald, & Langer, 1985) documents the occurrence of behavior within intervals on a 15-minute daily grid. It is especially useful in identifying times when challenging behavior is likely to occur. The boy's aggressive outbursts and noncompliance occurred primarily when the mother was attending to his younger brother or when she was preparing a meal. In assessing her interaction during these problematic times, the mother was always in a rush and was anticipating problems with her boys.

Our first intervention was to slow her down and program in some time for herself, and also some special time with her younger son. She was taught some relaxation techniques using BRT, and she practiced using them daily before problem times. Respite care was arranged for her boys to enable her to start doing things for herself again. The next intervention was to teach the mother how to structure leisure activities with her boys. During this time, the mother learned to reinforce and provide some structure during those problem times. As soon as the mother started feeling that she was back in control of her household, the inappropriate behavior of the older son started to decrease and the two boys started sharing toys and playing more appropriately with each other.

A 15-year-old young man was demonstrating aggressive behavior toward his 16- and 8-year-old sisters. The young man would not allow his sisters to go upstairs in their home without following them. Once the young man knew that his sisters were not going into his room, he would return downstairs. At times he would start yelling and screaming when he realized that his sisters were upstairs with him prior to his checking on their whereabouts. The young man would also become quite emotional if his favorite sports team did not perform well, to the point of being physically abusive to his sisters and mother. At the time of the initial assessment, the family was not allowing him to watch sports on television. This was very difficult to enforce because the household had cable and the father was also a sports fan.

The intervention used in this case was stress reduction paired with some self-talk (or anger control). The young man was asked to monitor his angry behavior and temper tantrums throughout the day. The mother was also asked to monitor his behavior. The mother was used as a reliability observer to verify that the young man was tracking his appropriate behavior. Prior to going to bed, the young man was given feedback on how he had performed that day. He was also taught behavioral relaxation training (BRT) during his session with the Project Ecosystem's counselor. Once he demonstrated acquisition of the ten behavioral postures, the counselor had the young man pair some self-talk with the BRT. The self-talk mainly consisted of the young man saying to himself: "Everything is going to be OK," "My sisters are just going to their room," and "There is always tomorrow for my team to do better." The BRT and the self-talk, along with the daily feedback provided by his mother, reduced his yelling and screaming and aggressive behavior to zero almost immediately.

The parents felt so comfortable with this type of intervention that they started asking their son to go into the living room and practice his relaxation whenever they felt he was becoming upset. On occasion, he would go into the living room and practice without a prompt from his parents.

A single mother with two sons, a 5-year-old and an 8-year-old who is diagnosed with autism, was concerned about her older son demonstrating considerable aggressive and noncompliant behavior. The major problem for the family was that the older son was not toilet trained and would urinate and defecate on the kitchen stove. The mother had tried to toilet train the child, but was unsuccessful. The younger child imitated his older brother and would escalate during a stressful time by being noncompliant or aggressive toward his older brother. The mother was having a difficult time managing both boys and working full time. During the initial assessment, the mother complained about a lack of free time and constant headaches upon arriving home. She was unwilling to collect data on the intensity and frequency of her headaches, but from her self-report during the interview she indicated that it was focused around household responsibilities that needed to be completed on a timely basis: getting the boys up for school, getting them dressed, putting them on the bus, picking them up from daycare, dinner, bath time, and bedtime. By the end of the day she always felt stressed or had a headache.

One of the first things taught to the mother was BRT. The mother had some difficulties following through with the procedure, but once she reached criteria she reported that she started feeling better and was able to go to sleep at night. Her headaches eventually started to decrease.

After the mother demonstrated acquisition of BRT, toilet training and structuring activities in the boys' daily routine were attempted. The toilet training procedure was very successful for the older son, and the structured activities with both boys enabled the mother to regain control. The mother reported that she felt she would have been unable to do the latter program if it were not for BRT intervention.

Henry was a 24-year-old resident of a group home. He displayed moderate mental retardation, autism, and was thought to have Fragile X syndrome. Henry was referred to Project Ecosystems because of tantrums, noncompliance, anger outbursts, and property destruction. He received training in BRT from a Project Ecosystems' counselor. After training in the relaxation postures, Henry was taught to count his breaths (a discriminative stimulus for relaxing) whenever he began to feel agitated. After this was put in place procedurally, the staff of the group home were instructed to reinforce his breath counting whenever he did it. As a result, the number of outbursts was considerably reduced, and when he exhibited a now infrequent outburst, the staff were able to gain almost immediate control and redirect Henry.

Susan was a 34-year-old female resident of the same group home. She, too, was referred for aggressive outbursts and tantrums. She was diagnosed with mild mental retardation and had a seizure disorder. The same BRT and breath-counting exercises were employed with Susan as with Henry, with similar results.

Stress reduction techniques have become staples of psychological intervention in the past generation. Behavioral relaxation training, deep muscle progressive relaxation, and biofeedback appear equally effective, each with its own advantages and disadvantages. We have found BRT especially useful with the clients of Project Ecosystems. We have used it with children with developmental disabilities, with attention deficit with hyperactive disorder, and with learning difficulties. With the children with ADHD and learning difficulties, we have had them apply it to situations in which they are easily frustrated, such as tasks they find very difficult. BRT has also been useful with explosive behavior in the children and adults we serve. We have received very good social validation from teachers and parents when we have used BRT with children. It has been especially gratifying that the children are able to generalize the skill to numerous situations and settings. This is not surprising, because it is such a "portable" skill.

In the ecobehavioral model, it is rare that only one treatment is employed with a family or a child. Such is the case with BRT. This procedure is useful in a variety of self-control problems; however, it must always be accompanied by reinforcement programs for compliance for practice and application of BRT, for learning to discriminate situations that bring on anger or frustration, and the need to teach care providers to arrange the environment to prevent aggression and frustration. Planned activities training and other methods described in this book are necessary adjuncts to BRT.

Summary

Parents who have children with developmental disabilities generally suffer from more stress than do parents of children without developmental disabilities. The demands of interventions may actually cause additional stress to a family seeking services. Thus, teaching stress reduction to parents is an important adjunct to other services, such as parent training. In this chapter, we have described the use of stress reduction techniques, especially behavioral relaxation training (BRT), to help parents better cope with the stressors in their lives and to help them when learning other programs, such as planned activities training. Additionally, we have successfully used BRT with children with a variety of disorders and with adults with developmental disabilities.

CHAPTER   SIX

Counseling and Problem Solving

When behavior therapy and behavior analysis became increasingly popular in the 1960s and 1970s, debates raged as to whether a therapeutic relationship was relevant between therapist and client in delivery of these science-based treatment procedures. The general notion in behavioral psychology was that because of its scientific foundation the therapeutic relationship concept traditional to psychotherapy was of little value in behavior therapy. With experience, however, behavioral psychologists discovered that patient numbers decreased if therapists failed to display warmth and understanding toward their patients. People may want the kind of direct help behavior therapy and behavior analysis offers, but they also want a sympathetic and empathic person delivering those services.

Teaching counseling skills to staff members is an important feature of an ecobehavioral program. These counseling skills are based on those espoused in humanistic psychology, but they have been task-analyzed by Borck and Fawcett (1982) and can be taught as systematically as any behavioral procedure. These skills include: active listening, reflecting, asking questions, summarizing, and teaching problem-solving skills.

Active Listening

Active listening communicates to a client that the therapist is aware of what the client has to say and how the client feels. When the counselor visited the Anderson family, Dave wanted the counselor to understand how very much Sean's behaviors have caused family stress in multiple ways. Cynthia wanted to communicate to the counselor how ambivalent she was about doing anything that could involve her less in the way of daily care of Sean; yet she was aware that she was not being particularly successful in dealing with his challenging behaviors.

To demonstrate active listening, the counselor assumes an active listening posture, maintains eye contact, uses facial expressions that convey listening, and makes nonverbal encouragements (Borck & Fawcett, 1982). The general posture for active listening involves sitting straight, holding the head up straight, placing the hands in the lap or on the arm of the chair when not gesturing (a good thing to do), and keeping the feet on the floor (not moving them). Eye contact is critical for active listening. We all know how uncomfortable it is to talk with someone who does not maintain eye contact. This is especially important for a counselor who must listen to the difficult problems of parents with children with developmental disabilities.

Similarly, facial expressions must reflect the content of the parents' concerns. Thus, when Cynthia Anderson describes to the counselor how difficult it has been to deal with Sean's aggressive behavior toward his sister, the counselor must show concern on her face. When Dave describes Sean's problems as having caused economic problems in the family, the counselor might show concern and some surprise.

A number of phrases can be used by counselors to express understanding (Gordon, 1975). Borck and Fawcett (1982) have suggested *uh-huh, I see, yes, oh, mm, yeah, mm-hm,* and *I understand.* We would also include *sure, you bet, I know, right,* and *really(?).* The quality of these verbalizations is also important; keep the tone nonthreatening while avoiding any semblance of sounding bored.

Observations by the counselor during active listening are very important. Borck and Fawcett (1982) outline four essential activities:

1. Identify the content of the client's verbal statements.
2. Identify the client's feelings.
3. Identify the feelings of the client's verbal behavior.
4. Identify the feelings of the client's nonverbal behavior. (p. 27)

When examining the client's verbal statements it is important to glean a "what," "who," "where," and "when" from the remarks. For example, Cynthia Anderson describes to her counselor that she is very frustrated with the developmental center Sean attends. The counselor needs to listen carefully for the "what." That is, does the counselor know what the developmental center is and what its program is supposed to do? Does the counselor understand the "who"? That is, with whom is Cynthia frustrated? Sean? The teacher? The director? The "where" may seem obvious, the developmental center; however, there could be specific problems with a particular classroom, the bus, or the playground. Finally, "when" involves identifying whether Cynthia is frustrated with the whole program, or just the early morning program, or just the program on certain days.

Identifying the client's feelings involves an important clinical skill— placing oneself in the client's place and asking: "How would I feel?" "Would this make me happy, sad, angry, scared, or confused?" (Borck & Fawcett, 1982). The tone and intonation of the client's voice should give the counselor salient clues about which descriptor fits. In our example, Cynthia cries as she describes her frustration. This gives the counselor a clear idea of how very frustrated Cynthia is. Other clues Borck and Fawcett have identified are: loud voice, soft voice, pause and sigh, talking very quickly or very slowly, laughing, and silences. They suggest that loud talk indicates anger. A soft voice may indicate fear or sadness. Pausing and sighing may reflect confusion, depression, or frustration. Nervousness, fear, or excitement is thought to be expressed through fast talking, whereas slow talking might suggest sadness or depression. Laughing may indicate happiness or nervousness, the latter usually being the case for Asian people. Finally, these authors have suggested that silences may indicate nervousness, depression, or confusion.

Cultural differences must be in the forefront of evaluations of these expressions by counselors. Counselors working for Project Ecosystems attend workshops covering cultural differences among the several ethnic and racial groups we serve.

Feelings can also be identified by observing body language. Borck and Fawcett (1982) identified a number of body movements and their associated likely feelings, such as nervousness or fear being expressed by trembling fingers, wringing hands, finger or foot tapping, or swinging the leg over the knee. They suggest that nervousness might be expressed by shaking a foot back and forth.

Sadness or depression can be observed with shoulders pulled forward, the head facing down, the eyes to the floor. This could also suggest shame, guilt, or embarrassment. Anger is often associated with pounding a fist or foot stomping. Confusion can be expressed by raising the shoulders toward the ears.

Reflecting

After observing the client's verbal and nonverbal behavior, the next important step is to reflect those feeling to the client. In our counselor's first meeting with the Andersons, Debbie said, "What would you say is the biggest problem you are having with Sean?" Cynthia replies, "I have lots of problems with him" (nervous laugh). "I'm not sure I can put a finger on a singular problem" (nervous laugh). Debbie then says, "you sound a little nervous about talking about this."

Later in the same session, after a pause and in a soft voice, Cynthia says, "As a matter of fact, Sean has created more problems for all of us than I would have imagined." The counselor replies, "You sound as though this really depresses you."

This kind of reflecting on the counselor's part helps the client recognize understanding and empathy from the counselor and opens the doors for communication that facilitates other more direct behavioral assessment techniques that may be employed with the family.

Asking Questions

The use of open and closed ended questions are further skills recommended by Borck and Fawcett (1982), and Project Ecosystems counselors learn these skills too. Open ended questions are used to open sessions. They serve to help the client help set the agenda. These questions are also used to ask the client to state a problem, for specifics, when the counselor notices sudden changes in verbal or nonverbal behavior, in helping a client refocus (that is, go back on-task in a discussion), and in examining alternatives during problem solving.

An example of an open ended question for opening a session might be as simple as the counselor asking, "How can I help you today?" In trying to identify specifics, Cynthia might have said, "Sean is a problem all the time." The counselor's response might be, "What do you mean by problem?" Follow-up on this can lead Cynthia to focus on specific challenging behaviors and their definitions.

Closed ended questions focus on facts. "When is that a problem?" "Where is that a problem?" These questions require facts for answers. Cynthia might say, "I have tried everything to get Sean to stop hitting his sister." A closed ended question from the counselor aimed at obtaining facts from Cynthia would ask, "Exactly what have you tried?"

Summarizing

Summarizing is another very important skill for the counselors to use during sessions. The counselor needs to help the client summarize the issues for each topic area. Summarizing statements, like the other issues discussed here, are not complicated. The counselor might say, "Let's go over Sean's challenging behaviors that you brought up today." In doing so, the counselor would use active listening to make sure he or she understands all of Cynthia's concerns about Sean's challenging behaviors, how Cynthia feels about those behaviors, and what the next steps will be.

It is very important to have the client confirm or dispute the counselor's summarizing statement. The counselor would ask Cynthia whether she felt that all the issues about Sean's challenging behaviors were addressed. This provides another opportunity for the counselor to use active listening skills to be sure the counselor and the client perceive the summary in the same way. If there is a lack of correspondence, the counselor must ask the client to correct the summarizing statement; the counselor might say to Cynthia, "What did we leave out regarding Sean's challenging behaviors?"

We have provided a basic outline of the Borck and Fawcett (1982) manual. For a thorough review, the reader is referred to that book.

Problem Solving

Good counseling skills are prerequisite to being able to teach problem-solving skills to the client. Examples of the kinds of problems faced by parents of children with developmental disabilities include finding an appropriate babysitter or careprovider for their child, finding a daycare center, working with the school to arrange the best possible individual educational plan (I.E.P.), or finding a physician or dentist for the child.

After the counselor has summarized the client's concerns (given verbally), and the client confirms that those are the concerns, the counselor is ready to request a problem statement. The problem statement helps the counselor and the client define the problem. In this case, the problem statement might be, "I am unable to find daycare for Sean." This focuses the counselor and the client on a specific topic. To better define the problem, the counselor might ask what type of daycare Cynthia is looking for. With this type of questioning, both the counselor and the client are defining the problem. Cynthia might respond, "Some place where Sean could go after attending the Developmental Center." Now the problem statement is, "I need to find a daycare that Sean could attend after going to the Developmental Center." The counselor needs to direct the problem statement into an action statement: "Where do I find a daycare that Sean could attend after going to the Developmental Center?" This sets up the problem-solving process.

The next step is to have the counselor explain the problem-solving process to the client. The counselor tells the client, "First, we must define the problem." In this example, the problem would be, "Where do I find a daycare that Sean could attend after going to the Developmental Center?" The counselor then explains the process of exploring as many options or alternatives to the problem as possible (brainstorming). Once we produce as many options or alternatives as possible, we can evaluate the consequences of each option or alternative by examining the benefits, problems, feelings, availability, and prerequisites in carrying out each one. After evaluating each option or alternative, each will be judged on its own merit as being poor, fair, or excellent. From these ratings, an option or a group of closely related options is selected. A plan is formulated to implement the option or group of options.

After explaining the problem-solving process, the counselor should emphasize the usefulness of the process. Doing the problem-solving process produces a variety of options that may not have been explored initially and might not have been explored at all without the problem-solving process. The counselor explains to the client that the process enables them to make better decisions and provides additional information that might have been overlooked initially.

Now that the problem-solving process has been outlined and the usefulness in doing the procedure has been explained, the next step is to identify as many options or alternative solutions as possible. This is the most important aspect of the problem-solving process. The counselor must be careful not to generate options or alternative solutions for the problem. The problem belongs to the clients; thus, options or alternative solutions must also be generated by the client. The counselor can guide using open ended questions, for example, "Where do Sean's classmates attend daycare?" This might prompt Cynthia to talk to Sean's classmates' parents to find out what they do about daycare. The counselor should encourage the client to produce as many options or alternative solutions as possible without making any evaluation of these options. If the client is unable to generate further options or alternatives, the counselor should use the open ended questioning format to assist the client: for example, "Do you know anybody else with the same problem?" The counselor should try to prompt the client to generate as many options or alternative solutions as possible. Five options or alternatives is considered a minimum.

Once the options or alternative solutions have been generated, the next step is to evaluate the consequences of each option or alternative solution. Examine the benefits, problems, feelings, availability, and prerequisites of each option or alternative solution. Before moving to the next option or alternative solution, the counselor should review what the client has said to verify that the consequences were correctly recorded.

Once the counselor and the client have evaluated each option or alternative solution, the client is asked to rate each one. The counselor does this by stating the option or solution and reading the client's evaluation. Once the counselor hears how the client evaluated the option or solution, the counselor requests the client to rate each as poor, fair, or excellent. After proceeding through each option or solution and attaching a rating, the client and the counselor will have a clearer picture of how to proceed in the problem-solving process to a solution.

The ratings enable the client to focus on what option or solution is best for his or her particular need. The client now selects an option or solution to implement. Once the selection is made, the counselor ensures that the client is satisfied before helping the client develop a timetable to implement the option or solution. During this phase, the counselor can role-play with the client to determine how to implement the option or alternative. This enables the client to establish an expectation and develop possible behaviors to handle any problems with the option or solution.

In concluding the problem-solving session, the counselor summarizes what was accomplished during the session. The counselor initiates the summarization by making a statement such as, "Let's review what we did today." This starts the closing procedure and also allows the client to review what went on during the session. The counselor continues by stating how the client presented the problem initially: "You were concerned about Sean and finding appropriate daycare for him. After going through the problem-solving process, you picked an option or solution to deal with your concern. You decided to contact some of Sean's classmates' parents to see what they are doing regarding daycare." The counselor should be in an active listening posture and demeanor should be neutral.

When the counselor finishes the summarization, a request for feedback is provided in the statement, "How do you feel the session went?" This provides the client with the opportunity to evaluate the session and give the counselor feedback on how the client feels about the outcome. The counselor then asks the client if there are any questions. Once again, this provides the client the opportunity to ask questions regarding any steps during the session or ask questions about what is supposed to be done in the near future. The counselor should answer any questions the client has regarding the session.

Before terminating the session, the counselor should schedule the next appointment by establishing the date, time, and place of the appointment. The counselor should confirm any expectations of the client by the next session; usually, some homework assignment has been given and implementation of a plan of action has been discussed. Before ending the session, the counselor should offer future help to the client if needed before the next appointment. For example, "You know how to get in touch with me if you need some help?" The counselor should make a closing statement such as, "I felt that the session went well. I'm looking forward to seeing you at our next appointment on Monday."

Case Studies

An example of problem solving with a Project Ecosystems' family involved a situation in which the parents of a student were concerned that the medication prescribed for their son was inappropriate. The parents felt that the school wanted the medication to suppress their son's behavior to the point where he would not be a problem in the classroom. The parents had to specify the purpose of the medication, not the effect of the medication. For example, "Why was my child put on medication?" The parents came to the understanding that their son was placed on medication to enable him to enhance his learning opportunities. Now the issue of medication needed to be addressed from that viewpoint. Was the medication, in fact, enhancing their son's learning capacity? In talking to the school and to their son's physician, the parents were concerned with one issue—enhancing their child's education. The school and the physician needed to address that issue also, instead of simply trying to control the boy's behavior through medication. Using the problem-solving process, the clients were able to focus their concerns and evaluate the possible alternatives.

Through problem solving, the parents learned how to express their concerns to the school personnel and receive answers to their questions. A compromise was achieved. Medication was used to enhance the child's learning, but not so much medication as to seriously dull his behavior. The family requested that the school allow the Project Ecosystems counselor into the classroom to advise the teacher on classroom behavior management. This occurred with a very successful outcome.

In the ecobehavioral model we describe, it is important to remember that none of the treatment procedures we detail are delivered exclusively or in a vacuum. Trying to solve problems such as daycare or choosing a physician who might have expertise with children such as Sean Anderson will not change Sean's challenging behaviors or teach the Andersons new skills in dealing with Sean. With this concept in mind, here is an example of problem solving combined with symbolic modeling in what could also be described as behavioral pediatrics.

Diane Coolwater (a pseudonym) was the 28-year-old single mother of four children ranging in age from 2 years to 11. Her circumstances were certainly different from the middle-class Anderson family. Diane had been a special education student as a child. Three of her four children showed developmental delays, and her 3-year-old son, Patton, not only had moderate mental retardation but had a congenital heart problem. The family lived on welfare in a trailer in California's high desert. They owned a 1969 model of a large American car that consumed so much gasoline that Diane could seldom afford to fill the tank.

Patton's cardiac condition had been noted by his family physician when Patton was 18 months old, and the physician told Diane that she would need to bring Patton to a large university hospital in Los Angeles for follow-up examinations and care each year. Six months after the physician told her this, Diane made an appointment at the university hospital, which was a 2.5-hour drive from their home in the desert. Diane had saved money for gasoline for the car, and when the day for the appointment arrived, Diane loaded the four children in it and headed for the hospital. She had been to Los Angeles only twice as an adult, but had never done the driving herself. Both times before had been with the fathers of her children and they had driven.

Diane found the freeways extremely confusing and got lost numerous times, stopping in gas stations to ask for directions. She became quite frightened when she found herself lost in what was clearly a bad neighborhood. The appointment had been for 11:00 A.M.; she had left the trailer at 8:15 A.M. They finally arrived at the hospital at 1:45 P.M. Once more Diane became very confused, this time in trying to find the correct parking lot. After finally finding the correct lot, she became flustered and embarrassed at not knowing how to conduct herself with the parking lot attendant. She did not know what to do with the ticket, or when to pay. This caused her considerable anxiety, something most people would never consider.

As Diane and the children tried to find the pediatric cardiac treatment unit, the children became extremely challenging because they were hungry. Diane was aware of how late she was for Patton's appointment, so she took no time to find food for the children who had become so disruptive that hospital personnel and others were staring at the Coolwater family. When they finally found the correct office at 2:15 P.M., the receptionist informed them coolly that the doctor had afternoon surgery and that there was no one to see Patton.

The fiasco of this trip was not over. At this point, Diane asked where she could find food for her hungry children. Directed to the hospital cafeteria, she was astonished at the price of food and was able to purchase sandwiches, drinks, and chips only for the children, leaving her without money for herself. She took a few bites from each child's sandwich. The Coolwaters left the hospital at 3:00 P.M. and after becoming lost again a number of times on the way home, arrived at their trailer at 7:30 P.M. with the children and Diane very hungry and the children entirely out of control behaviorally.

One year later, Patton's physician reported Diane to the child protective service for medical neglect because he determined that Patton had never been seen in Los Angeles for his cardiac evaluations. The child protective service referred the Coolwaters to a regional center for which Project Ecosystems is a vendor, and that regional center referred the family to Project Ecosystems.

The goal established by the regional center and Project Ecosystems was to teach Diane how to take Patton for his cardiac evaluations on an annual basis. The first strategies used were the counseling and problem-solving procedures we have described in this chapter. Out of embarrassment, Diane had never told any professional all the details of her disastrous trip to Los Angeles. The counseling strategies used by the Project Ecosystems counselor allowed Diane to feel comfortable enough with the counselor to finally describe all the difficulties of her attempt to take Patton to the hospital.

After listening carefully and showing empathy for Diane's difficulties and embarrassment, the counselor was able to launch into problem-solving strategies with Diane. Together, Diane and the counselor identified the following problems to overcome so Patton could receive the medical care he required: child care, so that Diane would not be burdened by the other three children during the trip to Los Angeles; money for food and gasoline; being familiar with the way to the hospital; overcoming Diane's embarrassment and understanding how the parking lot worked; and managing Patton's behavior during the long day.

All the strategies described in this chapter were used to help Diane create solutions to these problems. For child care, she made an agreement with a neighbor who had once offered to trade child care services. If the neighbor would take care of Diane's other three children on the appointment day, Diane would return the favor when the neighbor needed child care. The counselor and Diane decided the appointment should be made far enough in advance that Diane could put aside a little money each week to save for food and fuel on the appointment day, and this time to have a contingency fund saved so that if more meal money, phone money, parking money, or other expenses were required she would be prepared.

Symbolic modeling (Bandura, 1969) was used to show Diane how to get to the hospital and how to overcome her fear and embarrassment about parking. The counselor drove from Diane's trailer in the high desert to the hospital in Los Angeles, taking photographs of important salient stimuli on the way. Critical, of course, were photos of the relevant road signs, such as highway numbers and exits from the freeway. The counselor also took photos of the parking lot entrance and of a motorist pushing the button for a ticket. A parking lot attendant graciously posed for some photos of the sequence required to interact with her and smiled while doing so. This was done to allay Diane's concerns about feeling inadequate in this situation. Finally, the counselor took photos of the salient discriminative stimuli within the hospital, such as the arrows on overhead signs directing patients to the appropriate clinics. Also, the receptionist posed for photos showing her friendlier than she had been to Diane. One set of slides and one set of prints were made. The counselor showed Diane the slides in one session to make her comfortable with the entire route and to calmly answer any questions Diane might have. The prints were put in an album of single plastic pages that could easily be flipped consecutively for reference while Diane was driving.

Child management was handled by teaching planned activities training to Diane and having her especially adapt it for taking Patton in the car. Although this process may seem cumbersome, Diane made a very successful trip to the hospital with Patton. She felt quite accomplished. The counselor reported that she could veritably *see* the new self-esteem on Diane's face. Because Patton had not been seen at the hospital before, the physician there requested a follow-up visit three months later. Diane was able to plan this with little assistance from the counselor. After nine months with Project Ecosystems, Diane had enough new skills that her case was terminated by Project Ecosystems and four months later, after the second follow-up visit in Los Angeles, the child protective service dropped its neglect charges.

The counseling and problem-solving strategies used with Diane are similar to those used with several Project Ecosystems families. Although the problems differ greatly in content, the method used to solve them is virtually standardized. It is our belief that the high ratings we receive on social validation questionnaires (see Chapter 10), are largely due to the counseling skills our counselors display. These strategies so carefully outlined by Borck and Fawcett (1982) should be part of any ecobehavioral effort with families.

Summary

Implementing ecobehavioral services with families is only as good as our ability to establish a counseling relationship with them. Staff members of this and similar projects should be taught counseling and problem-solving skills. Good counseling skills involve active listening, reflecting, asking questions, and summarizing. Problem-solving involves helping the client and the family create a problem statement, explaining the problem-solving process, creating options and alternatives, rating the alternatives, and summarizing.

Also presented in this chapter were case examples showing the utility of counseling and problem-solving skills. On Project Ecosystems, these procedures, like all the others we describe, are used in conjunction with other ecobehavioral strategies.

CHAPTER SEVEN

Behavioral Pediatrics

The field of behavioral medicine is a relative newcomer, first defined in the late 1970s. The *Journal of Behavioral Medicine* was created in 1978, and its editors defined behavioral medicine as a relationship between health/ biobehavioral issues and applied psychology. A more strict behavioral definition was provided by Pomerleau (1979), who defined behavioral medicine as:

> (a) the clinical use of techniques derived from the experimental analysis of behavior—behavior therapy and behavior modification—for the prevention, management or treatment of physical disease or physiological dysfunction; and, (b) the conduct of research contributing to the functional analysis and understanding of behavior associated with medical disorders and problems in health care. (p. 655)

Behavioral medicine involves behavioral research and treatment applied directly to certain health problems, indirectly to others, and directly to broad-scale programs and problems. Examples of treating health problems directly would be behavioral treatment programs for weight loss, smoking cessation, and pain. Indirect treatment usually implies issues of compliance, such as having a juvenile diabetic comply to her diet, foot care, and urine testing regimens (Lowe & Lutzker, 1979); teaching asthmatic children to use inhalation equipment (Creer, 1970); teaching a child to swallow pills (Blount, Dahlquist, Baer, & Wuori, 1984); or preparing children for surgery (Twardosz, Weddle, Borden, & Stevens (1986). Broader issues would involve using behavioral strategies to teach medical personnel various procedures, such as a well baby examination protocol, or to examine procedures to reduce noncompliance to medical follow-up examinations in a family practice center (Rice & Lutzker, 1984).

The applications of behavioral medicine extend from prenatal issues through gerontological issues. Thus, as this field began to grow exponentially, a subfield was quickly born, behavioral pediatrics. Varni and Deitrich (1981) delineated behavioral pediatrics from behavioral medicine by the focus on behavioral pediatrics with children, development, and parent/child interactions. Expanding on this, Russo and Varni (1982) defined behavioral pediatrics as being:

1. interdisciplinary
2. concerned with the management of disease, related symptoms, and child management
3. rooted in empirical methodologies
4. concerned with long-term care, acute intervention, and prevention
5. data-based
6. involving ambulatory and inpatient environments
7. concerned with disease mechanisms and biochemical, physiological, and behavioral interrelationships (p. 15)

The techniques of behavioral pediatrics include operant conditioning and social learning procedures conducted through applied behavior analysis, cognitive procedures, and self-regulation procedures. Several of these strategies have been incorporated in in-situ treatment programs on Project Ecosystems. The case examples in the next section demonstrate the use of these strategies.

Case Studies

Ted was an 8-year-old boy with autism who displayed serious tantrums and would attempt elopement if he suspected his mother was taking him to the physician. Because of this problem, it had been an unacceptably long time since the child had a proper medical examination. Our attempt to treat this problem represents behavioral pediatrics involving indirect treatment—getting Ted to cooperate with going to the physician.

Accessible to Ted noncontingently was his favorite toy, Game Boy, a handheld computer game. The Project Ecosystems counselor made an arrangement with the mother and Ted that access to the Game Boy would now be controlled by the mother and that it would be accessible to Ted contingent upon his cooperation with a shaping/modeling program the counselor developed.

From descriptions by the mother of the scenarios that seemed to upset Ted most about going to the physician, a hierarchy was created not unlike fear hierarchies created for other phobias treated by systematic desensitization. The hierarchy created for Ted consisted of seven steps:

1. Step out of the car, and step in again at the doctor's office.
2. Touch the door of the doctor's office building.
3. Touch the elevator door inside the hallway of the doctor's office.
4. Take the elevator to the second floor.
5. Touch the door of the doctor's office.
6. Go inside the doctor's office.
7. Complete step 6 without the counselor.

The first step in this treatment program was to establish imitation as a reinforcer for Ted. The counselor spent time in the home modeling several simple motor behaviors for Ted. Contingent upon imitation, Ted received a few seconds' access to his Game Boy. After two sessions of this simple imitation training, several more complicated behaviors were modeled, such as standing by the car and getting in the car. After two sessions of these behaviors, the steps in the hierarchy were modeled, again with imitation being reinforced by access to the Game Boy. The hierarchy was completed in seven sessions. During each of those seven sessions, approximately 25 models were presented. Ted imitated each without further prompting.

After the seventh session, Ted accompanied his mother without incident for a physical examination at the physician's office. In this case, simple modeling, imitation, and reinforcement procedures were used to address a serious behavioral pediatric problem.

Another example of indirect treatment of a medical fear involved a 7-year-old girl with Down syndrome who would vomit in anticipation of a physician's appointment. The child, Ann, had a history of medical problems and needed medical examinations on a regular basis. In conducting a behavioral assessment, the Project Ecosystems counselor interviewed the mother. She reported that Ann would cry, scream, and vomit every time she was to go to a medical appointment. The mother reported that Ann's fear had generalized to the sight of blood, even on television, walking in oozing mud or puddles, or grass clippings. The mother told the counselor that if Ann was watching television and someone in the program was depicted as going to a medical appointment, the child would cry and scream.

The counselor arrived at the home to observe the family prior to a medical appointment. Because Ann had appointments at least once a month, it was not difficult to schedule these observations. During the counselor's visit, the mother prepared the car for the trip. She covered the back seat with a white sheet, and wrapped Ann in a sheet. She brought along a wash cloth to use for any cleaning up that was needed.

Of course, by doing this it was apparent that the mother had created operant and respondent stimuli further setting the occasion for and eliciting the vomiting. By respondent conditioning, we mean that formerly neutral stimuli, such as being in the car, were now paired with nausea and had thus become conditioned stimuli that elicited feelings of nausea. By operant conditioning, we mean that the mother's comments and placing the sheet in the car set the occasion for the daughter to become nauseated. In fact, this is a good example of how serious disorders can develop through these two conditioning processes and where a clear line between operant and respondent conditioning cannot always be drawn.

As the mother drove to the doctor's appointment, she would repeatedly ask Ann how she was doing and how she was feeling. If Ann started to become upset, the mother would plead with her not to get sick. This would make Ann more upset, to the point of causing her to cough and spit. The mother would then pull over and wipe Ann with the wash cloth and tell her that everything was going to be all right. Upon arriving at the physician's office, Ann would begin to calm down. The mother reported that this was a typical experience in driving to a medical appointment.

The counselor asked the mother whether Ann ever became worse than this. The mother reported that one time Ann had the flu and she actually vomited all over the back seat, which is why she covered it and Ann with sheets.

From what the counselor viewed during this observation, it seemed to be a stimulus control issue. The white sheet and preparation for the trip to the doctor's office seemed to be setting the occasion for Ann to cry, scream, and spit (not vomit). The counselor wondered what would happen if the mother did not prepare the car and the child for the doctor's appointment in such a manner. As luck would have it, a week later, Ann was playing at a neighbor's home when she fell of the swing set and injured her arm. The mother did not have enough time to prepare the car for the trip to the emergency room. Ann showed none of the usual behaviors on the way to the hospital. When reviewing the incident with the mother and discussing preparations to go to a follow-up appointment, the counselor explained to her that she could bring toys or favorite items with which she and Ann could interact during the car ride. The mother had a difficult time understanding the procedure or how it would help. The counselor role-played with Ann in the home, pretending they were going in the car to see the physician. The first time, the counselor pretended to be the mother and Ann played herself. Then they switched roles, and Ann got to drive the car, playing the mother while the counselor played the child. The counselor then asked the mother to participate in the role-playing. Both the mother and daughter enjoyed pretending to go to the physician's office.

The following week, the mother had to take Ann for a follow-up visit for her broken arm. The counselor asked the mother to use activities that she had role-played with the counselor during the car trip to the appointment. The counselor was unable to go with them, but the mother later reported that Ann did not cry or scream; as a matter of fact, Ann laughed and enjoyed playing with her mother during the drive.

When the counselor asked whether mud and fresh grass cuttings still created difficulties for Ann, the mother reported that it was no longer a problem. The mother reported that she had often mentioned to Ann that getting wet or muddy sometimes leads to illness and more medical visits. The mother no longer mentioned this regarding playing outside.

Michael was a 9-year-old boy living in a foster home. He was referred to Project Ecosystems because of his limited attention span and inability to work on tasks. His foster parents did not know how to structure activities to motivate Michael to stay on-task. The Project Ecosystems counselor visited the school and the home to observe Michael. During the observation at school, Michael was able to stay on-task for 30 minutes while playing dress-up with the other students. During the structured academic time, though, Michael demonstrated the same type of off-task behavior that the foster parents were reporting.

The counselor knew that Michael had the ability to function in an activity as long as he was having fun or being provided with feedback or stimulation. The counselor structured an activity in which Michael would be able to discriminate lower- and uppercase letters and, given that he did not know how to spell his name, learn to do so. Using these two target skills, discrimination of letters and spelling his name, the counselor designed a card game in which Michael received points for matching the same type of letters. He could use these points to earn free play with the counselor or with the foster parent. Once the letters were separated, Michael was asked to spell his name using the lowercase letters.

Michael enjoyed playing the game. The foster mother reported that Michael began generalizing to other words in his environment—milk, water, and food. Michael would take out the carton of milk and spell the word *milk* with the playing cards. At school, his teacher said Michael had become more attentive and showed more willingness to follow directions.

As Michael showed progress in the treatment from Project Ecosystems at home and in school, his medication came up for review. His psychiatrist reviewed his file and changed his medication and dosage. The foster parents did not question the change in medication for Michael. During the first night of the new medication, Michael suffered a serious adverse reaction to the medication. He was awake all night with hallucinations. The foster parents were unable to reach the psychiatrist, so they called another psychiatrist. The new psychiatrist prescribed another drug for Michael without instructing the foster parents to discontinue the other medication. Now Michael was receiving two different types of medication from two different psychiatrists. He became nearly catatonic and was unresponsive to all requests. The foster parents became alarmed. Michael was sleeping more and remained unresponsive to their attempts to interact with him. They were worried that if they discontinued one of Michael's medications, his challenging behaviors might escalate.

The Project Ecosystems counselor engaged in problem solving with the foster parents to make up a list of alternative solutions to address the medication problem. The foster parents finally returned to the original psychiatrist to discuss the medication problem and its side effects. This enabled the foster parents to make an informed decision regarding his medication. After about one month of adjusting Michael's medication, he regained his skills of working on-task for long periods of time, discriminating letters, and spelling his name.

The foster parents reported to the regional center that had they not known, prior to the medication change, that Michael was able to work on-task, they might have attributed the medication reaction to Michael's usual behavior patterns. Because of the Project Ecosystems counselor's work with Michael and the foster parents' new knowledge of what he could do, it was obvious to them that something was wrong.

Juan was a 4-year-old boy who had recently been placed in foster care. His dietary habits were problematic. He would eat only snack food, potato chips, peanuts, and popcorn. He refused to eat any meat, vegetables, or fruit. His foster parents were concerned, as was his physician, because Juan was losing weight. Juan was referred to Project Ecosystems because there was no medical reason for his weight loss, but it was becoming a medical problem.

After conducting a behavioral assessment, it became clear that Juan would refuse food from his natural and foster parents until he was given snack food. Juan would refuse food for two days, creating a medical emergency, and the foster parents would be forced to provide him with some type of food that he would eat.

The behavioral assessment also indicated that Juan enjoyed eating dry cereal without milk. The counselor created a contingency whereby Juan could earn some cereal for a bite of vegetable or meat. The counselor began offering a taste of a vegetable or meat for a bowl of cereal. Manual guidance was required to aid Juan in getting the nonpreferred food into his mouth. The amount of vegetable or meat required to earn the dry cereal was slowly increased. In one month, Juan was eating equal amounts of meat and vegetable independently to earn the dry cereal.

The most difficult part of the program was the beginning. It took considerable effort to get Juan to try the meat or vegetable. Another difficulty was getting his natural mother to try the new feeding program. She had visitation rights, and she would feed him snack foods so she would have a more enjoyable visit. This always caused problems for the foster mother later at mealtime. Juan wanted nothing to do with vegetables or meat after his natural mother's visits. The Project Ecosystems counselor taught the natural mother how to perform the feeding program. The child protective service agency cooperated by making the mother's length and type of visitation contingent upon her compliance with the feeding program. Once the natural and foster parents were both implementing the program, Juan showed a marked increase in his progress with the feeding program.

Direct treatment of a life-threatening self-injurious behavior, tongue biting, has also been successful. Mickey was 2 years old when he was referred to Project Ecosystems. He had profound developmental and physical delays, suffered from seizures, and was nonambulatory. Mickey grasped objects only when they were handed to him, partly because of several visual impairments. He lived in a foster home.

The specific referral from the regional center was to reduce Mickey's screaming, hand biting, and tongue biting. There was a legitimate concern that the tongue biting was so severe that he would either bite it off or swallow it and choke to death. Thus, there was a plan to have all of his teeth removed if we could not remediate this seriously challenging behavior. The only previous attempt at treating the hand biting was to keep Mickey in arm splints so he could not get his hand into his mouth.

Our functional assessment showed that reinforcers appeared to be physical touch from adults, sound, attention, and bright objects that he could hold very close to his face. Based on the functional analysis, it appeared that the self-injurious behaviors occurred for two not mutually exclusive reasons: one for attention, the other related to seizure activity.

Treatment involved a version of planned activity training, simply engaging Mickey and making reinforcers contingent upon engagement. To engage or stimulate him, Mickey was placed in different positions and objects were made available to him within his reach. Through manual guidance and fading, he was taught to use a spoon and ultimately to feed himself. Use of the spoon and engagement with objects were reinforced with touch, praise, bright objects, additional attention from the counselor and, later, from the foster mother.

Using these reinforcers and through shaping, Mickey was taught to scan his immediate environment and to reach for objects placed near him. Through increased engagement, the time spent wearing the splints was systematically and gradually reduced. For putting his hand in his mouth when the splints were off, or for the mouth movements that were associated with tongue biting, the counselor said, "STOP," and withheld attention and objects for one minute.

These engagement, reinforcement, and simple time-out procedures were effective in eliminating the tongue and hand biting. The use of the splints was eliminated. These procedures were also taught to the special education teachers, and the results were replicated in the school Mickey attended.

One more example of direct treatment of a medical problem is failure to thrive. These eating disorders can produce serious life-threatening problems for children. Such was the case with a child referred to Project Ecosystems for a severe disorder. Kelly was 5-years-old when she was referred. She displayed only mild developmental delays; however, she was grossly underweight because she only accepted milk from a bottle. She possessed simple signing skills and had poor fine motor coordination.

It had been speculated that Kelly might actually have a veritable phobia to eating because of having choked on solid food at one time. When she was referred to Project Ecosystems, she had been seen by an occupational therapist who had tried to force feed her. This resulted in Kelly screaming, crying, choking, and holding food in her mouth for hours at a time.

Our functional assessment determined that there were a few foods that Kelly would tolerate. Using a discrete trial method, Kelly was presented with a small amount of a favorite food. If she swallowed, she was praised and allowed momentary access to her bottle. As the number of trials in which she accepted food increased, nonpreferred foods were introduced and preferred foods were used as reinforcers, replacing the bottle. Gradually, access to the bottle was eliminated altogether.

As progress was made with the use of foods, similar training was accomplished by teaching Kelly to use a cup. Initially, she was given water in the cup. Later, water was gradually replaced with weak apple juice, then full-strength apple juice. Similarly, she was given weak grape juice, followed by full-strength grape juice.

During food training and cup/liquid training, the counselor gradually reduced the number of trials on which she worked with Kelly, simultaneously introducing the mother to conducting the trials, until ultimately the mother was conducting the entire session with the counselor watching and providing encouragement. Finally, as Kelly gained eating skills, weight, and new communication skills, the counselor arranged for Kelly and the mother to ceremoniously throw away her bottles. Also, she was moved successfully from a crib to a bed, and the counselor taught the mother how to use toilet training skills with the child, which were successful in a matter of days.

Monitoring the effects of medication is another aspect of behavioral pediatrics. The direct observation methodologies of applied behavior analysis and the use of single-subject research designs are helpful in examining the effects of psychotropic medication for children served by Project Ecosystems. For example, Ted was a 9-year-old boy diagnosed with mild mental retardation and attention deficit disorder with hyperactivity (ADHD). His parents received parent training from Project Ecosystems, but the neurologist who referred him was interested in learning whether or not methylphenidate would serve as an adjunct to the ecobehavioral treatment Ted and his family were receiving. Thus, baseline observations were made in school and home directed at assessing Ted's fidgeting and off-task behaviors. Following baseline, Ted's behavior was monitored for one month during and after his parents received parent training. The neurologist placed Ted on daily doses of methylphenidate. The data showed that parent training alone had a modest but clear effect in improving Ted's behavior and that the medication further enhanced Ted's performance at school and at home.

In other cases, we have worked with neurologists and have demonstrated that various medications have had no or negative effects on child behavior. The children were removed from these medications or had them changed. Direct observation in the child's natural settings has been very useful in monitoring the effects of medications. It can also be used in diagnosis. For example, when no stimulant medication has any positive effect on behavior, it can be concluded that ADHD may be an improper diagnosis.

As can be seen from the case descriptions provided here, behavioral pediatrics is an integral part of a comprehensive ecobehavioral approach to families who have children with developmental disabilities. In attempting behavioral pediatric programs, it is essential that appropriate medical personnel be involved in the relevant aspects of the program.

Summary

Behavioral pediatrics is a subfield of behavioral medicine that focuses on behavioral applications to the medical problems of children through indirect and direct treatment of medical problems. Examples in this chapter include case studies involving failure to thrive and other eating disorders, conditioned nausea and other medical fears, and monitoring the use of psychotropic medication. Behavioral pediatrics is a natural element of an ecobehavioral model because of the collection of direct observation data and the focus on in-situ observation and treatment.

Basic Skills Training

The very term *developmental delay* justifies the need to conduct basic skills training for an ecobehavioral program serving children with developmental disabilities. The reasons for referral to Project Ecosystems are that a child displays behavioral excesses or behavioral deficits, or both. A child suffering behavioral deficits has problems at home, in school, socially, and in virtually any setting in which the child behaves.

Children with developmental delays display those delays in one or more of these realms: personal self-care, social behavior, communication, safety, and academic and preacademic skills. Examples of personal self-care deficits include toileting skills, hygiene (toothbrushing, wiping, bathing), self-dressing, and feeding. Social skill deficits may include a lack of normal social amenities, such as saying "hello" and "good-bye" and so forth, appropriate affect, matching affect and emotion, and the lack of generative social verbal behavior. More complex social deficits might be in the area of community living skills, such as how to order in fast food restaurants, how to behave in workshop or school settings, how to play with peers, and sexual behaviors.

Communication deficits include a lack of any communication skills, limited signing skills, or limited verbal skills. Safety deficits often involve a lack of awareness of street safety or street-crossing skills. Other issues of safety around the home include the accessibility of poisons, dangerous electrical outlets, firearms, and other suffocation items, such as nonedible items on which a child might choke or plastic garment bags on which a child might suffocate.

Preacademic skills in need of assessment and treatment often include lack of attending/attention skills, color discrimination, size discrimination, letter recognition, scissor skills, and other fine motor skills possessed by developmentally normal kindergarten or first-grade children. Academic skills include reading, arithmetic, and social studies.

The critical feature when working with clients on many of these skills within the ecobehavioral model is to teach these skills in natural settings whenever possible. For example, Project Ecosystems has a day program for adults who have not succeeded in other day programs because of their behavioral excesses and deficits. Only 1½ hours per day are spent in our office/teaching site working on social and other skills. The remainder of the day is spent in the community, teaching community living skills directly in the settings in which those skills are needed. Some of the skills taught in the natural community setting are bus riding, restaurant behavior, shopping, and street crossing.

Case Studies

Henry

Henry was a 4-year-old boy diagnosed with mild developmental delay. He lived with his mother, father, and brother. He was referred to Project Ecosystems for lack of attention skills, toilet training, and behavioral and medical noncompliance. The medical noncompliance involved his refusal to wear braces on his feet at night, which had been prescribed to correct an orthopedic problem.

The functional assessment noted that Henry would engage in tantrums whenever his parents placed demands on him. The assessment also determined that likely reinforcers were social contacts, videos, candy, liquids, and a variety of toys.

Behavioral noncompliance was treated with two strategies: compliance training and planned activities training (PAT). Compliance training involved teaching the parents to give simple commands to Henry and reinforce compliance with a different reinforcer each time from the long list of reinforcers determined by the functional assessment. The Project Ecosystems counselor also asked the parents to gradually increase the frequency of commands they gave to Henry each day. Further, from the functional assessment the counselor had determined which commands were more likely to produce compliance, noncompliance, or a tantrum. From that information, a hierarchy was created. The parents were asked to progress from giving commands that had the greatest likelihood of compliance to those that had less likelihood, and finally to those that had previously set the occasion for a tantrum. This process took approximately six weeks.

Concurrent with compliance training, PAT was initiated with the parents. Because of their work schedules, the father spent more time with Henry than the mother did, although she spent evening time with him. Both parents were cooperative learning PAT, which took six weeks to teach.

After the six weeks of compliance training and PAT, Henry's compliance to commands changed from 5 percent to 85 percent. The parents reported enjoying PAT, and as so often appears to be the case with PAT, they reported being able to take Henry to numerous community sites they had avoided previously, such as movies and shopping malls.

A fading program and role-playing were used to get Henry to wear his orthopedic device. Prior to treatment, whenever the parents put on Henry's brace, which attached to both legs and connected them and made him uncomfortable and fairly immobile, he would cry, scream, and kick violently. Henry was supposed to wear the device while sleeping each night, so the parents would wait for Henry to fall asleep and then place the device on him. He would usually wake up screaming within an hour or two, and the parents would remove the device.

The role-playing involved having Henry wear the device for a few minutes during regular visits by the counselor early in the evening, long before his bedtime. For this compliance, he received a reinforcer he had chosen from his list. The fading program involved having the parents place the device on Henry while he was asleep just prior to his normal time of awakening in the morning, having them wait in his room until he woke up, and then immediately removing the device and provide him with a reinforcer. The goal of his program was twofold: to reinforce compliance, and for the parents to gain control over removal of the device contingent upon compliance rather than tantrum. Each day the counselor asked the parents to awaken themselves earlier so they could place the device on Henry. At the beginning of the program, "earlier" meant 15 minutes. The parents were willing to disrupt their own sleep schedules because this involved much less disruption than the lengthy tantrums they had endured.

After this fading of time was moved successfully to three hours prior to Henry's awakening, the counselor asked the parents to try to put the device on Henry before he went to sleep. (The role-playing had continued, and he was regularly being reinforced for having the device on when he awakened.) This produced immediate success, and Henry began sleeping the entire night while wearing the device. The parents, Henry, and the orthopedic surgeon were pleased with the results.

A toilet training program necessarily involves a degree of compliance by the child. The child must be able to follow simple commands and have enough fine motor skill to pull up and down clothing, and to empty a potty. Given that Henry had deficits in these skills prior to treatment, the counselor deferred toilet training until the compliance training was effective. Then the counselor spent a few sessions with Henry and his parents teaching him finer coordination. Henry was taught to pull his pants up and down on command. Compliance was no longer a problem; however, manual guidance was needed to teach this skill. The manual guidance was gradually faded.

Rapid toilet training as described by Azrin and Foxx (1974) was used to toilet train Henry. Few modifications in the protocol were needed. Modeling with a doll, prompting by liquid "loading," reinforcement, and positive practice were used. The modification was that rather than trying to conduct the procedures over a four-hour period, as is recommended by Azrin and Foxx (1974), the training was carried out in five one-hour sessions over five days. After training, Henry had only two accidents and quickly became fully daytime toilet trained. Generalization to nighttime occurred within days of the completion of daytime training.

This case is an example of the use of several components of the ecobehavioral approach to produce important and durable changes in a family's ecosystem. The parents were quite pleased with the results of these interventions, and Henry displayed considerable pride in his new behavioral accomplishments.

Susan

Susan was a 9-year-old female resident of a foster home. Her diagnosis was early infantile autism with related distractibility. Further, it was noted that she had difficulty in communication, displayed motor stereotypy, and had diagnostic features of Rett syndrome and Lennot-Gastant syndrome. Susan was referred to Project Ecosystems because the foster home was licensed for ambulatory clients only and that licensing was going to consider Susan nonambulatory because she was noncompliant in fire drill practices (Bigelow, Huynen, & Lutzker, 1993).

One aspect of functional assessment is to conduct reinforcer sampling. This was accomplished with Susan by exposing her to a variety of foods and toys and having the counselor record the items Susan showed the most interest in by taking, eating, or playing with them. The care provider conducted the same assessment three times in a week. Food, praise, and a Mickey Mouse doll were shown to be the most effective possible reinforcers.

Fire drill training involved saying "fire" to Susan and asking her to walk outside, something she would never do prior to training nor during baseline. A simple changing criterion design was used to demonstrate that shaping and reinforcement were effective in teaching her to go outside for fire drill. This involved beginning with having her move just a couple of steps toward the door after the "fire" cue was given. For compliance, she received praise, food, and access to the doll. After a few sessions, only praise was used, as Susan showed considerable enthusiasm for her progress toward the goal. For nine sessions the number of steps required toward the door was gradually increased until she went all the way outside the door with no further prompts. This treatment was remarkably simple, and the outcome was most productive for Susan and for the foster home, as licensing then qualified Susan as ambulatory and she was able to stay in the setting.

Lupe

Lupe was a 10-year-old boy with autism who was referred to Project Ecosystems because of a lack of attention skills, noncompliance, daytime and nighttime enuresis, and lack of safety skills. There was particular concern because Lupe would run into the street with no apparent regard for traffic. He lived with his 7-year-old sister and his parents. The father worked in construction, and the mother stayed home with Lupe.

This particular case is another good example of the interrelation among ecobehavioral services offered by Project Ecosystems. For example, while safety was of paramount concern, the problem was related to noncompliance and to the mother's lack of engagement with Lupe. Thus, the Project Ecosystems counselor began teaching the mother to engage in compliance training with Lupe. The mother learned to give simple commands and to provide contingent reinforcement for compliance. The functional assessment had determined that attention, video games, and fruit were reinforcers for Lupe. These items were used contingently and in variety as reinforcers during compliance training.

After a few sessions of compliance training, Lupe's rate of compliance had increased from near zero to over 60 percent. The counselor then began working directly with him, taking him to the front yard and telling him to stay there. At first, Lupe was reinforced for not running after one minute. Concurrently, the counselor had Lupe engage in a simple activity such as swinging on the front yard swing for that one minute. This was to teach Lupe to engage in an activity that would be incompatible with running in the street. The mother observed this training. As the time that Lupe played was lengthened, the counselor began having the mother instruct him and provide reinforcement.

As this process progressed, the mother was provided with PAT, which taught her the general notion of engagement. During each visit, the counselor had the mother create a weekly "lesson plan" of activities with which she would engage Lupe. Prior to these programs for Lupe and his mother, he was running into the street an average of 12 times per week. After the training was completed, Lupe stopped running into the street altogether.

Attention training began with the counselor sitting at a coffee table across from Lupe, who sat in a small chair. The counselor held Lupe's hands down and asked him to look at her. After no response, it was necessary for the counselor to manually guide Lupe's face to face hers. This was reinforced with a small cut up piece of fruit. Gradually, the counselor was able to fade her manual guidance and have Lupe orient toward her by the verbal prompt only. Once Lupe was able to attend on command, training switched to token training for correct attending and for the performance of simple tasks.

Both parents were taught how to use the token economy, and as a part of problem-solving training the counselor actively programmed generalization of the parents' skills. This was accomplished by telling the parents to generalize (Stokes & Baer, 1977). The counselor would review skills the parents wanted to teach Lupe and would discuss issues of compliance and challenging behaviors the parents wanted to eliminate. Each discussion covered only one of these issues, but the counselor reminded the parents that they knew how to use token reinforcement. Thus, the counselor provided cues to the parents to try to generalize. Evidence of this generalization occurred after the fourth problem-solving session. Without prompting the parents described how they had incorporated tokens into two other skill programs with Lupe. Throughout the remainder of the sessions with the parents, they showed similar generalization.

After working with this family for nine months, no further treatment was necessary. Lupe was no longer running into the street, and he had developed several new skills that allowed him to be moved into a different special education class than the one in which he had been enrolled. In the new class, a curriculum was developed to advance Lupe through new skills in which he would now be able to engage because of the changes that had occurred during his treatment from Project Ecosystems.

Dana

Dana was a 15-year-old male client who lived with his parents. Dana had a compulsive behavior of following his 13-year-old sister upstairs to make sure she did not go into his room. Whenever his sister went upstairs, he would get up from wherever he was sitting and follow her. If she stopped near his room, he would begin yelling and threatening her. His parents were concerned because on some occasions he would actually hit her. They were also concerned that their daughter felt trapped in her own house.

The Project Ecosystems counselor conducted a functional assessment and found that Dana would follow his sister upstairs under almost all circumstances unless he and his father were watching sports on television. The counselor conducted another assessment on Dana's sports watching habits. These results showed that Dana was an avid sports fan, and when his favorite team was doing well, he could contain his anger. However, if his team started to lose, he would yell and throw objects such as couch pillows and shoes.

The counselor decided to work on Dana's anger control by teaching him BRT (behavioral relaxation training). The counselor worked with Dana in the living room, going through ten different positions. Once Dana acquired the skills to relax himself, the counselor introduced sports programs on television by watching sports events with him. If Dana began losing control of his temper, he would be instructed to begin his relaxation training. His parents would request that Dana go into the living room and practice his relaxation exercises before continuing to watch his sports program.

Dana was trained to monitor his anger while watching sports. If he threw anything or started yelling, he was taught to start breathing slowly and to subvocalize, telling himself to relax. The counselor role-played with Dana during this teaching procedure. During the role-playing, the counselor explained to Dana what he needed to do. The counselor then demonstrated the procedure to Dana by pretending to be him and letting Dana, who was pretending to be the counselor, cue him when to start the relaxation procedure. After Dana provided the counselor with accurate feedback on when to initiate the relaxation procedure, they switched roles. Dana practiced doing the procedure with the counselor, who provided feedback.

Once this phase was mastered, a TV sports program was introduced. Dana and the counselor would watch baseball or basketball. Dana was asked to monitor his behavior during the program. This was very difficult for him because he would become totally involved in the sports action and forget to monitor his behavior. With practice using the cue to relax, he became more aware of his behavior and showed an improvement in his ability to control his anger.

The counselor started having Dana's parents track his behavior while he watched televised sports. The parents would, upon occasion, cue Dana to practice his relaxation. If he lost control by throwing an object or starting to scream and yell, he was told to turn the television off and practice relaxation in the living room. The parents reported that within two weeks Dana was able to watch sports without throwing objects or screaming or yelling. The parents reported that on occasion Dana initiated relaxation training by turning the television off and going into the living room to practice.

The next intervention was a similar procedure used for sports programs. Dana was still in the habit of following his sister upstairs to check on her whereabouts. The counselor told Dana to practice his relaxation procedure while counting slowly to 20 and saying, "Everything is going to be okay." Dana and the counselor engaged in the same role-playing procedure as before, with Dana playing the counselor and the counselor playing Dana. They switched roles after Dana established the appropriate cues. After Dana had demonstrated the required behaviors, the counselor enlisted the help of Dana's sister. The counselor told Dana's sister to mention to her mother that she was going upstairs so that Dana could overhear the conversation. The counselor monitored Dana's behavior and only prompted Dana if he started to skip any of the predetermined steps. After only a few sessions, Dana was able to stop following his sister upstairs once he realized that she was probably just going to her room or to the bathroom.

Both of these procedures were successful because of Dana's ability to learn the relaxation procedure and to follow some concrete steps to control his anger. Dana's parents continued to monitor his behavior for televised sports and following his sister upstairs. They mentioned that they were very pleased with Dana's improvement, but that a new problem needed to be addressed. The parents were concerned that Dana would not shave in the morning before going to school. This caused some problems because he had a part-time job at a local fast food restaurant after school, and the manager of the restaurant indicated that Dana would arrive at work looking disheveled.

The counselor asked the parents to monitor all three behaviors: following his sister upstairs, watching TV sports, and shaving in the morning. The counselor and Dana went upstairs to the bathroom to observe how Dana shaved. Dana had an electric shaver but did not move it correctly along his face. The counselor then demonstrated how to use the shaver correctly. Dana practiced and initiated the counselor's model. Dana quickly learned proper shaving techniques.

By this time, the counselor and Dana had developed a very positive relationship. Therefore, a contract was created with Dana stipulating that if he could reach four out of seven days per week of meeting the criteria of no tantrums during sports events, leaving his sister alone, and shaving, he and the counselor would go out for ice cream. If he did not reach these criteria for four out of seven days, he would be required to practice his relaxation and shaving procedures (simulated) for the duration of a training session (one hour). Dana's parents continued monitoring his behavior. The parents posted the data sheet on the refrigerator door so Dana could check it every day after dinner to see how he was doing. Dana's mother noted that occasionally he would become agitated if he disagreed with what was on the data sheet. The parents would cue Dana to practice his relaxation training. He would comply and soon regain control of his behavior. Gradually, the criteria were changed to six out of seven days per week. The parents were satisfied with these criteria, and reported that it was more enjoyable to interact with Dana. The parents were pleased with his ability to control his own anger and to shave independently in the morning. The employer also reported satisfaction with Dana's improved performance.

This case demonstrated how a procedure such as BRT helps a client gain more control over his own behavior with very little intervention on the parents' part. The parents only needed to monitor Dana's behaviors and to provide prompts when he needed some assistance with his own self-monitoring. Not all Project Ecosystems cases require so little intervention on the parents' part. Sometimes, much of the families' life-style needs to be modified to achieve a modicum of success.

John

John was a 15-year-old young man with severe and multiple handicaps, including visual impairments. He had no language skills, very little hand or leg movement, and could not perform skills independently. He was referred to Project Ecosystems because he constantly rubbed his shoulder to his ear, causing large sores on his ears. During the initial assessment, the parents reported that on occasion John would insert his finger in his eye or severely pound on his ear with a closed fist. Upon asking the parents for more information about the circumstances around which these behaviors were occurring, it became apparent that it was when John attempted to communicate to his parents that he was not feeling well. It was found that these behaviors occurred when John had a very high fever or an infected ear. Once these symptoms were appropriately addressed, John ceased the self-injurious behaviors.

The counselor decided to teach John some basic survival sign language. Rubbing his chest and then pointing meant "I want this, please"; just rubbing his chest meant, "please." Because John's parents and his teacher at school had never seen John initiate these kinds of behaviors, the counselor was not sure that John would initiate any of her models to sign. Because he never responded to any stimulus farther away than two to three feet in front of his face, it was believed that that was as far as he could see. The parents were skeptical about this communication program. The counselor decided to begin the program on a trial basis, since both the counselor and the parents were unsure whether John could perform the tasks.

The communication program was based on John being able to sign "please" for every spoonful of food during mealtime. John did not self-feed, thus his parents had to feed him. Now John was required to sign "please" before each spoonful. The procedure went as follows. The counselor asked, "John, do you want some food?" He was physically prompted to rub his chest and was given the spoon by his parents. Upon receiving the spoon, John was provided with physical guidance to scoop, at which time the parents would say, "scoop." Next, physical guidance was used to guide the spoon to John's mouth. The spoon was then placed down on the table. The task was broken down into four components: signing "please," picking up the spoon, scooping and putting food into his mouth, and returning the spoon to the table. Each component was recorded to identify the type of prompt needed to complete each step. The type of prompts given were physical assistance, gesture, verbal, or independent. Mealtime was used because it provided a natural time each day during which the training could occur.

For the first two weeks, John had to be physically prompted through the entire procedure. During the third week, he started moving his hand without some physical assistance. At this time, the counselor taught the parents to imitate the counselor's role. The parents also began working with John during breakfast. Now John was receiving training twice daily, breakfast and dinner. During the following two weeks, John's parents reported that he required very little physical assistance to feed himself and was now signing "please" without any assistance whatsoever.

The counselor implemented a delayed prompting procedure in requesting, "John, do you want some food?" The parents were instructed to hold the spoon up and say, "John, do you want some food?" They were told to wait three to five seconds to see whether he would sign "please." He did sign "please," and the parents faded to simply saying, "John," which cued him to sign "please."

As John became more proficient at signing "please," the parents and the counselor decided to see whether they could get John to make choices. Two items were offered at once. John was asked to sign "I want that, please" by rubbing his chest and pointing to what he wanted. The two items offered were the spoon and a cup of yogurt drink. Initially, this confused John, but he soon demonstrated that he could make a choice. To say that John's parents were pleased is an understatement. They could not believe how far John had progressed within such a short period of time. The most exciting news came one weekend when John's older sister visited her parents. The sister, who had never had any communication with John, was eating a banana. She turned to look at John and noticed that he was rubbing his chest and pointing to the banana. The sister and the parents were very enthusiastic over this generative communication. This was the first time John had generalized "I want that, please" other than at mealtime. John was also responding to someone with whom he had received no direct training. At this point, the parents requested that the school no longer manually feed John, and requested that the training program from home be carried out in school. The teacher was taught the same procedure used in the home, and within a few days John began responding to activities and to other children in his classroom.

Self-injurious behavior was the initial reason for John's case being referred to Project Ecosystems. However, we could not justify conducting a behavior reduction procedure without first adopting a positive program.

Because the self-injurious behavior functioned as a type of communication, the counselor needed to identify a more appropriate means of communication for the client. John had no verbal skills, so sign language was chosen as a form of communication. John's self-injurious behavior was eliminated almost immediately after medical treatment was sought for his ear infections and once the structured programming began. John's parents were very pleased with the progress John made and were instrumental in the amount of success their son achieved.

Kareem

Not all cases referred to Project Ecosystems deal with home-based treatment. Sometimes cases are referred for work-site issues. Many of Project Ecosystems' young adult clients work in sheltered workshop settings. Such was the case of Kareem, who exhibited aggressive behavior toward other workshop employees and was unable to meet shop standards for productivity.

The counselor conducted a behavioral assessment of Kareem in the workshop. It was determined that he would become upset if he perceived other employees making fun of him and would then avoid work by wandering off-task. The supervisor for Kareem's work station typically paid attention to him only when he was off-task or causing problems with other employees.

The counselor met with the station supervisor and designed a program that would reinforce Kareem for being on-task and also engage the entire workstation in increased productivity. The program had two phases. First, the day was divided into 45-minute periods with a 15-minute break between each period. During the 45-minute work period, the station supervisor would walk around the workstation providing social reinforcement to any employees who were on-task and producing the contracted items. At the end of the 45 minutes, the supervisor would count the number of items produced within the time period, and if an employee produced enough items to meet the criterion, a coupon was given for a soft drink at the snack bar. Each employee was given recognition for being on-task and meeting criteria. The employees included in Kareem's workstation almost doubled their productivity.

A token economy represented the second phase. Now, the employees had to earn two tokens (plastic chips) before receiving a coupon for a soft drink. During the first phase, a baseline rate was established for each employee. The supervisor continued to walk around the workstation providing praise for being on-task and commenting about the employees' productivity level. The employees appeared to enjoy the positive interaction between the supervisor and themselves. What generalized from these interactions were more positive comments among employees.

At this same time, Kareem was receiving training in social skills from the Project Ecosystems counselor. The counselor modeled how to approach other employees and make "small talk" and how to make positive statements about other individuals. Kareem and the counselor role-played during the 15-minute break at the workshop. This provided the counselor with the opportunity to observe Kareem during the 45-minute work period. The counselor would ask Kareem to demonstrate his newly acquired skills during these 45 minutes of work. If he performed the skills correctly, the counselor would purchase a soft drink for Kareem during the next break. If he did not perform the skills, the counselor and Kareem would practice the skills during the break. Kareem earned his soft drink every time.

The counselor began fading his participation in this manner after six weeks. During this time, Kareem's productivity was above criterion and he did not demonstrate any social problems as long as he had work to do. When the workshop was between contracts, the employees were requested to sort and match nuts and screws. Kareem found this task boring and often caused problems by walking away and making disruptive comments.

The Project Ecosystems counselor introduced a contract to Kareem whereby he could earn a lunch out with the counselor if he performed to criterion for his productivity and social skills for a predetermined period of time. He did very well with this contingency. The Project Ecosystems counselor recommended to the workshop supervisors that some community integration be done during this "down time" between contracts. The employees found sorting nuts and screws very boring and this was an excellent diversion. This occurred and helped eliminate Kareem's and others' challenging behaviors during these periods.

This contract is an example of an intervention outside the home whereby the counselor only needed to contact the parents for consent for Kareem to leave during lunch. The workshop station supervisor was the mediator of behavior change in this case. After this treatment, the station supervisor felt more in control of his area. Additional employees were added to Kareem's workstation, and it became the station used to increase productivity of otherwise low-productivity employees. Once new employees entered the work area and experienced the incentive program that had been developed, their productivity level typically reached criteria of the group quickly.

In review of the case studies presented in this chapter, one common factor is found; challenging behavior was only addressed after established or appropriate incompatible behavior was systematically taught. By conducting functional analyses, clients' needs and adaptive behaviors are identified that can provide functional equivalence to the challenging behaviors for which the clients were referred.

Summary

Having developmental disabilities necessarily means delays in some basic living skills, social skills, educational achievement, or self-care. Basic skill training within the ecobehavioral model involves teaching these skills in situ and involves teaching others, such as parents, teachers, and siblings, to teach and maintain the skills with the family member with developmental delays. The case studies reviewed here exemplify the multidimensional nature of the ecobehavioral model and describe training in homes and in workplace settings. These case examples also demonstrate that when skills are taught it is often unnecessary to even consider a behavior reduction program. When new skills are learned, challenging behaviors often abate or disappear.

CHAPTER NINE

Staff
Training

The history of behavior analysis has its strongest roots in applications in developmental disabilities. The earliest work in the 1960s involved development and refinement of procedures. In fact, the 1960s could be described as the decade of procedures in applied behavior analysis. In the 1970s and beyond, the issue became one of how to teach others to effectively apply these procedures that were showing such great promise, especially with individuals with developmental disabilities.

In teaching parents, the question was, "What format is the most productive?" The conclusion here is that the most fruitful strategies are ones we know promote generalization. This includes teaching parents loose principles, naturally maintaining behaviors, and using the ecobehavioral model to create a family ecosystem that promotes and supports productive behavior change.

Several strategies for teaching staff have emerged over the years. It is clear that written or oral instruction alone is not very useful (Katz & Lutzker, 1980). Whenever these strategies are compared to more "hands-on" approaches involving modeling, role-play, and feedback, they are always shown to be inferior. The basic formula for teaching staff that has emerged is that first the staff member reads written information and passes a quiz on its content. Then, in simulation, a protocol or procedure is demonstrated to the staff person and that person is asked to imitate the model. Positive reinforcement is given for correct imitation, and corrective feedback is given for failure to imitate the model. A criterion should establish how many imitations should occur without a model before the procedure is considered to be learned by the trainee. After a trainee shows that the requisite skill has been learned, the next step is to conduct fidelity checks (quality assurance) in treatment settings. For example, after a Project Ecosystems trainee has been through several workshops on planned activities training and has observed a supervisor conduct PAT in a home, that trainee is then observed in homes conducting PAT and feedback is provided by the supervisor. We also make heavy use of videotape in supervision. When supervisors are not able to directly observe counselors, home sessions are videotaped so these sessions can be reviewed in supervisory sessions.

A Brief History of Staff Training

A variety of behavior management procedures have been described in trying to increase or improve staff performance. But few descriptions are available for teaching new skills to staff. Quilitch (1975) creatively examined extant administrative procedures to other strategies. He compared staff/patient interactions in a public residential facility, looking at these interactions across a variety of conditions. After baseline interactions were observed, the chief administrator issued a memo to staff asking for more staff/patient interactions. This, of course, is not an uncommon procedure in any setting; however, also not surprising, the memo had no durable effect on the frequency of interactions. The next step was that workshops were provided to staff on how to conduct activities with patients. This effort, again a common one in many settings, produced a transient increase in the number of staff/patient interactions.

The only clear and durable increase in staff/patient interactions came when a publicly posted board was placed on the units, and staff were asked to list the activities they planned to engage in with patients each day. This antecedent behavior management technique produced significant increases in interactions. Although the *quality* of the interactions was not examined in this research, it provided a good example of the use of applied behavior analysis methodology to examine existing administrative procedures and suggested a form of stimulus control (public posting of planned activities) to increase the frequency of staff/patient interactions.

Social reinforcement from supervisors (Brown, Willis, & Reid, 1981), self-recording (Burg, Reid, & Lattimore, 1979), and the use of instructions (Kissel, Whitman, & Reid, 1983) have been used with varying degrees of success when trying to increase or improve staff performance. An important added dimension to staff management was provided by Greene, Willis, Levy, and Bailey (1978). Instead of placing contingencies on increases in the amount of staff/patient interactions, consequences were provided to staff for improvements in patient *behavior*. Thus, quality rather than quantity became the variable of interest in the Greene et al. (1978) research. Considerable patient improvement occurred when these contingencies were put into place.

Again, it is clear that hands-on training must occur for other than conceptual learning to take place (Katz & Lutzker, 1980; Ziarnick & Bernstein, 1982). It is also important to validate the procedures to be trained. For, example, as described in Chapter 4, Lutzker et al. (1985) asked different experts, such as early childhood educators and preschool teachers, what affective skills adults should possess if they are going to interact professionally with children. And Newman (1989) found that it is necessary to train teaching skills to staff independent of the behavior management skills that they may need to learn. That is, if staff are going to be teaching behavior management skills to others, they must learn to use modeling, role-playing, and feedback in their own teaching repertoires. McGimsey (1987) also found this to be the case.

Project Ecosystems Staff Training

Staff Structure

Project Ecosystems has a three-tiered staff structure: doctoral-level trainers and supervisors, counselors, and trainees.

Doctoral-level trainers and supervisors Each doctoral-level trainer/supervisor is responsible for staff members in a given region. That supervisor conducts staff meetings, training, and supervision and is also responsible for maintaining relationships with each Regional Center whose service area is included in the supervisor's region. The supervisor is also responsible for fiscal matters pertaining to the Regional Centers, such as billing. Each of the doctoral-level supervisors meet together on a regular basis in management meetings, dealing with fiscal matters, training and supervision issues, clinical issues, and research. Supervisors discuss cases they are supervising. These discussions often produce treatment ideas that are passed on to the respective counselors for implementation.

Counselors Counselors are the direct service providers for Project Ecosystems. They provide the in-situ services in homes, schools, and so on. To become a counselor, a staff member serves as a trainee for three to six months, depending on the incoming experience and the background of the trainee. Counselors receive weekly supervision from the doctoral-level supervisor. The mode for supervision is face-to-face in the office; however, supervisors make many home visits with the counselors to maintain quality control of the services we deliver. We also make extensive use of videotape. Even though a supervisory session may be office-based, it often involves mutual observation of tapes made in situ by the counselor.

Counselors are paid for their face-to-face encounters with our clients and their families, including trips to schools and other community settings. Further, counselors receive a monthly travel reimbursement. Most counselors remain with Project Ecosystems until they finish their current academic program and are ready to move to a full-time career position or to a new graduate program. Each counselor receives a formal evaluation every four months, and all staff receive feedback from social validation questionnaires mailed to families after services are terminated.

Trainees Trainees are hired with the understanding that their training period is a probationary period, at the end of which trainees are evaluated for promotion to counselor or asked to leave the project. It is a period of mutual probation in that this is the time when the trainee evaluates whether she or he wishes to remain with the project and become a counselor. Trainees essentially serve an apprenticeship with a counselor. In addition to the specific training described below, trainees visit homes and other settings with the counselor, observing the counselor work with the families and assisting in data collection and simple activities with the children. During the apprenticeship, responsibilities are gradually increased for the trainee until the trainee is assigned an independent case. When this occurs, it is initially under the direct immediate supervision of the doctoral supervisor. Only when the trainee demonstrates sufficient independent skills and is promoted to counselor does this staff member ever visit a family without direct supervision.

Training Components

Staff training for Project Ecosystems combines the influence of past research dealing with staff training with our ecobehavioral philosophy. Skill training of staff always involves the following components:

1. reading material
2. writing a test with a must repeat until pass criterion
3. role-playing with a supervisor in a simulated setting

4. feedback from the supervisor until role-playing by the staff member reaches a performance criterion
5. observation by the trainee of the counselor applying the skill in a treatment setting
6. supervised application of the new skill
7. independent performance of the skill in the treatment setting with periodic video or direct observation supervision

These strategies are employed to teach trainees counseling and problem-solving skills, planned activities training, behavioral relaxation training (including use of videotape training), reinforcer sampling techniques, and functional communication skill training. Further, similar procedures are used to teach staff how to do rapid toilet training (Azrin & Foxx, 1974) and to work with nighttime enuresis.

For most trainees, the staff training process for Project Ecosystems begins with the trainee learning to conduct reinforcer sampling and functional communication with an institutionalized resident of a state facility. The state offers this facility for training opportunities for Project Ecosystems trainees and the residents of the facility. The training is provided to the state residential facility by Project Ecosystems without remuneration. Concurrently, as a trainee is learning these skills, he or she is attending staff meetings and making home visits with a counselor. Additionally, before or after staff meetings, the trainee is being put through the training procedures outlined above, first reading materials and being tested, and then going through simulation training before being allowed later to practice these skills with families. The training period usually lasts from three to six months before a decision is made to promote the trainee to a counselor position.

Staff meetings represent a critical element of staff training for Project Ecosystems. It is our belief that staff meetings should always provide a professional growth experience. They probably more resemble a graduate seminar than a typical staff meeting. Each week, a staff member reviews a previously assigned article, being asked to review its salient features and to describe how the contents of the article are relevant to work on Project Ecosystems. The subjects may be research, a clinical description, or a theoretical idea. After this, one or more clinical presentations by staff members are made. Actual assessments and treatments from current cases are presented. The purpose of these clinical reviews is to give staff experience in presenting cases in a professional manner, but more important, the purpose is to expose other staff members to clinical issues that may be different from those in their own cases. Together, we then problem solve issues of treatment. In addition to these presentations and reviews, we occasionally have a guest lecturer who might present research, treatment, or agency issues, such as changes in child abuse reporting laws, rights for individuals with developmental disabilities, or multicultural differences.

The only full-time staff members serving Project Ecosystems are the doctoral-level supervisors. All other counselors and trainees are part time and are students or recent students waiting to enter graduate programs. The nature of the work is quite demanding and entails considerable travel. We believe that full-time staff are not likely to give as much to each case as we expect. Therefore, we feel that developing professionals represent the best staff members for this kind of service. In fact, we are outright skeptical of anyone who wishes to do this work full time.

Several factors make students effective staff for Project Ecosystems. First, they are at a stage in their professional development in which they are excited about "helping" people, and they are able to do so. Also, in addition to the modest remuneration they receive, working for Project Ecosystems allows them to gain experience at a level not always available to graduate students. Many students are able to use Project Ecosystems as their practicum or internship site, earning course credits for their work. Thesis and dissertation research is also conducted by staff members of Project Ecosystems; in fact, such work is strongly encouraged. Further, we encourage staff to attend and make presentations at local and regional professional meetings. All these experiences are developmental for the individual staff member and serve the project well in helping to professionalize the staff.

Of course, utilizing students as direct service providers has some inherent problems. Their youthful appearances often cause a parent to question how much help the young counselor might be. Furthermore, a common question from parents to our staff is whether the counselor has children. If the answer is no, which is usually the case, a parent may again question whether the counselor can possibly understand the difficulties that arise from being a parent.

Preparing counselors in advance for these scenarios is the best way to deal with them. The first response to one of the queries of concern from parents is for the counselor to make use of the counseling skills that have been taught. Active listening and reflecting can be very useful. For example, the counselor may say, "It sounds as though my age (or my not having children) is of concern to you." Through this method, the parent has an opportunity to openly express concern. Having done so without argument from the counselor, the parent is more open to hear the counselor's reaction.

In response to parents' concerns, counselors may say, "I am younger than many parents and that, in fact, could limit my skills as a counselor in some ways; however, let me tell you about how I am trained and supervised." After describing training, the counselor might also add, "And let me assure you that if I am unsure of how well we are doing at any time, I will make a special effort to consult my supervisor."

We have consistently found students to be superior staff members despite their youth and relative inexperience. It is, nonetheless, very important to bear these issues in mind.

It is our strong belief that staff training needs to be developmental and continuously revised. Supervision and training are the keys to quality services. Thus, on Project Ecosystems, we prefer to regard our staff as junior colleagues who add to our professional development as we add to theirs. Finally, through social validation (described in more detail in Chapter 10), we are able to assess how the consumers of Project Ecosystems' services perceive the quality and outcomes of these services.

Dissemination

The ecobehavioral model differs from traditional mental health models of treatment. In some states it may differ from the manner in which services are provided to citizens with developmental disabilities. Thus, a question of dissemination is appropriate. That is, to what degree can this model be disseminated in such a way that it can be replicated elsewhere? For example, is it possible to use staff who are not students? What are the costs of such a model? These are important issues for consideration of possible replications of this model.

In describing the history and development of Project 12-Ways, Lutzker (1984) noted that the model cost one-half of a traditional mental health model. Of course, this is largely because of the use of students. Project Ecosystems costs approximately $30 per hour. This is much lower than most other services provided within mental health or developmental services models. Additionally, the California Commission on Developmental Services noted that collateral costs for other services provided by the regional centers were reduced for families that received services from Project Ecosystems.

Replications can take the form of grant-funded projects in association with departments of psychology or special education at universities. Such replications are certainly cost-effective for co-sponsoring agencies because only small amounts of their budgets are affected by such efforts. The cost for a participating agency may be nothing or it may require a match, usually not exceeding 25 percent of the grant.

The next question is whether or not an agency can replicate this model under its existing structure without using students as staff or without a grant. It is our belief that this model can be readily adapted to such a system. One of the purposes of this book is to outline training and organization of the model in such a way as to make replication a possibility. The staff training procedures we outlined earlier in this chapter should be used for staff of any human service agency.

Currently, ongoing replications of this model in services for individuals with developmental disabilities and for programs aimed at the treatment and prevention of child abuse and neglect are proceeding in Oregon,

Florida (2), Mexico, and Australia. Thus, the model has, in fact, begun to be disseminated. An analysis of systematic replications that compare efficacy with comparison programs delivered through agencies rather than through universities would be of great interest and value.

Summary

Staff training and development is a critical element of the ecobehavioral model. Staff training should always stress "hands-on" components and should focus on professional development. Our ecobehavioral model relies heavily on the use of student-staff. We offer several rationales for this and discuss some of the inherent pitfalls of this approach along with some solutions to the concerns of using student professional staff.

Can this model be replicated? We believe that is not only possible but desirable. Several attempts at replication are currently under way. An assessment of these programs will be looked forward to with great interest.

CHAPTER TEN

Evaluation

The distinguishing feature of applied behavior analysis and behavioral psychology is the focus on empiricism. Such is also the case with an eco-behavioral model. This is reflected particularly in the "analysis" aspect of applied behavior analysis. The goal of work in this area is to be able to assert with confidence that observed behavior change is a function of the manipulation of the independent variable(s), the treatment, and not the result of other spurious events that occurred at the same time.

If we see considerable improvement in the child's behavior after implementing planned activities training, can we be sure that these changes are a function of PAT? Or, could they be due to something else that happened in the family ecosystem at the same time that PAT was introduced? The change could be due to the child being concurrently enrolled in a special education preschool in which he or she began receiving intensive communication training, or it could be due to a major change in the family ecosystem, such as an older brother going away to college, a new housekeeper, or any of many similar scenarios. To have confidence that the change is the result of the treatment, data collection is necessary. When possible, simple research designs should be employed that have been created to show the functional relationship between the treatment and changes in the child's behavior.

It is critical to point out that collecting data and using simple research designs in real applied settings such as families and schools is much easier said than done. The elegant research data published in our best journals are difficult to replicate when conducting a large-scale community effort such as Project Ecosystems. The data we see in journals often reflect the work of a graduate student who has been funded through an advisor's research grant. There are several aspects of this "luxury" that allow the "clean" research we see in the journal. For example, grant funds allow the principal investigator or experimenter to hire and train reliability observers for data collection. Thus, two independent observers (recorders) collect direct observation data. In these research efforts, good, robust research designs are applied because of the research nature of the project.

In projects for which the funding is primarily service and there is often a clinical exigency, neither funds nor time are often available for reliability observers. Similarly, time constraints may hamper efforts to utilize the most desirable research design. A situation may present itself to Project Ecosystems whereby a multiple baseline design across settings (for example, school and home) might be desirable. This would mean that treatment would occur in only one of those two settings, while baseline data would continue to be collected in the other. Only when clear change occurs after treatment in the first setting would the same treatment be implemented in the second setting. However, the caseworker has made it clear to the counselor that immediate treatment is expected in *both* settings, precluding the staggered introduction of treatment across settings that is required by the multiple baseline design. Situations such as this make research design difficult in practical applications.

Accountability in Research Design

The difficulties in conducting thorough, clean research in applied settings notwithstanding, four methods of accountability should be attempted in all applied projects such as Project Ecosystems (Lutzker, Wesch, & Rice, 1984): clinical case studies or single-case experiments, research using single-subject designs with more than one subject or family, group designs, and finally, program evaluation.

Clinical Evaluation

At the simplest level is clinical evaluation. There is great value in collecting data whether the data are ever used in published research or even if there is a lack of reliability data. Clinical data serve several purposes. First, they can be used to show family members progress or lack of progress on efforts they are making. A counselor might ask Cynthia Anderson to record the number of tantrums Sean displays each day. Collecting this information and having the counselor present it in graphic form can be quite valuable in providing support and feedback to the parent. Furthermore, these data may serve another purpose, and that is the positive effects of reactivity; the mere act of collecting data may influence the individual collecting the data. This may not be desirable when employing independent observers to collect data for a research project, but reactivity with a parent can cause that parent to focus on efforts to change. In collecting tantrum data on Sean's behavior, Cynthia might be more prone to remember to praise more frequently and to engage him in activities as the counselor had recommended. Similarly, if the counselor had Cynthia track how often she criticized Sean, the act of collecting the data could reduce the frequency of criticism.

Clinical data are very useful in reporting to agencies and schools. Graphic data showing whether treatment goals have been met with a family provide an invaluable additional dimension. Finally, clinical data are very useful in supervision. When a counselor meets with a supervisor, clinical data provide a picture of progress or lack thereof so the supervisor can readily provide feedback to the counselor and make treatment recommendations. Many of the brief case descriptions we have provided in this book are based on clinical data collected by our Project Ecosystems counselors.

Single-Case Experiments

The second level of evaluation is single-case experiments or case studies. Kazdin (1982) has eloquently described the relevance of case studies and recommended parameters for when they should be published. A case study is a very thorough procedural description of a single clinical case. The best case studies contain the kind of clinical data we have just described. To be published, these thorough procedural descriptions should detail very dramatic outcome of long-standing challenging behaviors or skill deficits that have been unresponsive to treatment previously or simply problematic for a very long time.

The other prerequisite for publishing case studies, according to Kazdin (1982), is when the treatment is novel. For example, a published case study from Project Ecosystems described using functional equivalence training to reduce severe challenging behavior by an 8-year-old boy who virtually held his parents hostage through his violent lengthy tantrums and property destruction (Campbell & Lutzker, 1993).

Dan was diagnosed with autism. Some of his tantrums would last up to four or five hours. As is often the case with children such as this, the reason for the tantrum can be frustration at an inability to communicate. Then, of course, the tantrum is inadvertently reinforced by the parent and, in fact, the parent begins to inadvertently teach the child to escalate the tantrums. This seemed to be the case with Dan and his family. The Project Ecosystems counselor had the family record the length and duration of tantrums and list property destruction. The primary treatment, however, was indirect. Dan was taught several functional communication skills by the counselor, and later this training was gradually switched to the parents. From the beginning of training, there was a reduction in both sets of challenging behaviors. By the 11th week of training, the tantrums and the property destruction had disappeared.

This effort clearly met Kazdin's criteria for a case study in which a rather novel treatment was used to dramatically change seriously challenging behavior that had become protracted and treatment refractory.

Single-case experiments utilize a single-subject research design with one subject or one family. The two most common single-subject research designs are the withdrawal design and the multiple baseline design. The hallmark of all single-subject research designs is collection of repeated measured data. That is, data are collected over many sessions, days, or trials to ensure a clear picture of individual behavior. In a withdrawal design, baseline data (often referred to as condition "A") are collected over time until they are stable and give a clear picture of behavior in its untreated state. If the goal of a behavior change intervention is to increase behavior or performance, such as child compliance to parental commands, and the baseline data show performance to be declining, it is permissible to begin an intervention in the absence of stable data. Conversely, if the goal of an intervention is to decrease behavior, such as tantrums, and the baseline data show an increase in tantrums, it is similarly permissible to begin the intervention in the absence of stability.

The goal of all research designs is to show a functional relationship between the independent variable and subsequent changes in the dependent variable. Thus, in applied work, as we noted earlier in this chapter, the goal of a research design is to show that the treatment (often referred to as condition "B") was responsible for the change in behavior rather than the result of other events that happened to occur concurrently.

Even if there is a clear change in behavior between the baseline and treatment conditions, there is not yet sufficient evidence that the change is due to the treatment, because experimentally we have not controlled for time and other events that could also explain the change. Thus, an AB research design remains what we have called a case study. To create a robust design that shows the functional relationship we seek to demonstrate in a withdrawal design, treatment is withdrawn long enough to show that without it behavior returns to near baseline levels of occurrence. Thus, if a child were receiving token reinforcement for in-seat behavior in a special education classroom, the tokens and their back-up reinforcers would be removed for a brief period of time. This ABA design now shows that treatment is responsible for the changes observed in behavior. However, clinically this is not a desirable nor ethical outcome. Thus, the treatment is reinstated, creating an ABAB design, which is even more robust than the ABA in that it shows that treatment is responsible for the change and for maintenance of the behavior change.

A withdrawal design is only used with treatments that can be briefly withdrawn without harm to the subject. If a child is taught language using reinforcement and imitation procedures, it would probably be impossible to remove treatment. The natural environment reinforces language; so even if the structured treatment were somehow removed, the subject is still likely to use the newly learned language skill.

When a withdrawal of treatment does not pose an ethical or practical concern, it could be argued that failure to engage in a withdrawal creates an ethical problem. That is, the use of this kind of research design allows the clinician to have confidence that it is, in fact, the treatment procedures that are responsible for the behavior change and not some other variables. Failure to use a withdrawal design leaves questions as to the necessity of the treatment procedures; thus, the use of this and other single-subject research designs are arguably of the utmost ethical responsibility.

A withdrawal design was used fortuitously in a single-case experiment reported by Campbell, O'Brien, Bickett, and Lutzker (1983). They treated a mother and her 4-year-old daughter who had ADHD. The mother had reported a fear that she was going to kill her daughter because of her inability to manage the child's behavior. Two other factors complicated the situation. First, the mother suffered from disabling migraine headaches; second, the marriage was dysfunctional.

Prior to conducting what turned out to be successful parent/child training, the counselor felt it was necessary to treat the mother's migraine headaches. The rationale for this was that it seemed unlikely that the mother would be able to cope with the demands of the parent/child training when she was having such serious headaches. Thus, with the recommendation of a neurologist who had been unable to relieve this woman's headaches through medication, in-home relaxation and self-monitoring training was provided to the mother. The relaxation training involved deep muscle relaxation. The self-monitoring involved having the mother record situations that seemed antecedent to the tension that preceded headaches. She then was supposed to relax when she noted these situations. These two treatments had produced a dramatic reduction in headaches and in intensity of headaches after a brief baseline period. To that point, this was an AB case study. However, seeing the success of the program, the mother decided to try to get along without the self-monitoring. This brief "withdrawal" period brought a quick return of the headaches. She was instructed to return to the self-monitoring, which rapidly reduced the frequency of the headaches again. This inadvertent withdrawal design produced convincing evidence of the efficacy of the self-monitoring procedure in the treatment of migraine headaches. Child compliance training for the mother and subsequent marital counseling were additional components of this ecobehavioral approach that dramatically improved life in this family ecosystem.

Multiple Baseline Design

As we have just noted, a withdrawal design frequently does not serve a practical purpose. Fortunately, the multiple baseline design was developed to solve many problems posed by the use of withdrawal designs. A multiple baseline design involves introducing treatment staggered over time. This design can be employed across behaviors, settings, or individuals. For example, using a multiple baseline design, an illiterate mother with moderate mental retardation was taught to shop for nutritious meals (Sarber, Halasz, Messmer, Bickett, & Lutzker, 1983). Using match-to-sample procedures, she was first taught to shop for foods in the meat and protein food group. In the meantime, baseline data were still being collected on her shopping skills for the other three basic food groups. When the data showed acquisition of shopping skill for the protein group, she was then trained to shop for foods in the vegetable and fruit group while baseline data were still collected for the other two groups. This process continued until she was trained to shop for all four food groups. The logic of this design is that if a change in behavior is noted only when the treatment is introduced, then we have confidence that the changes seen are a function of treatment and not something else that has happened at the same time.

This shopping skill study was a multiple baseline design across behaviors (food groups). An example of a multiple baseline design across individuals would be if, as is the case with several families served by Project Ecosystems, there were a brother and a sister in one family in need of treatment. Both for research purposes and for clinical practicality, we first train the mother to use PAT with the boy. After she has mastered the skills with him, we would introduce the same treatment with the sister, having collected baseline data on the mother's and the daughter's behaviors in the interim. Again, if we saw a change in mother/child interactions only after treatment was introduced for each child, we would be confident that the change was a function of PAT. This would be a multiple baseline across individuals.

In Chapter 5, we described the use of BRT to reduce hyperventilation that preceded seizures in a boy with severe mental retardation (Kiesel, Lutzker, & Campbell, 1989). In that study, treatment was first introduced in the home, while baseline data continued to be collected in the school. When it was clear that BRT had reduced hyperventilation and seizures at home, the same treatment was introduced at school, where similar change was noted. Again, it was clear that BRT was responsible for the change in both settings, demonstrated through a multiple baseline across settings.

The multiple baseline design is a robust single-subject design that obviates the need for a withdrawal. It controls for time and extraneous variables as alternate explanations for observed behavior change. Its only limitation compared to the withdrawal design is that the multiple baseline does not demonstrate that the treatment is needed to *maintain* behavior change. The withdrawal design can show that the treatment is necessary for maintenance.

Single-case experiments such as those just described demonstrate with confidence the efficacy of a treatment or treatment "package." Although external validity of the procedures cannot be claimed because we are dealing with only one case, the internal validity of these research designs allows us to recommend with confidence that others try to replicate the procedures in other settings or with other subjects.

Assessing Generalization

Research with more than one individual or family allows for more conclusions about the generality of a treatment program. An example of this is the research conducted on planned activities training with Project Ecosystems families (Harrold, Lutzker, Campbell, & Touchette, 1992; Huynen & Lutzker, 1992). Clinical observation with several families cause us to believe that PAT might be as useful as contingency management training (CMT) in improving parent/child interactions. Previous research (summarized in Sanders & Dadds, 1993) had suggested that PAT could enhance outcome of CMT with parents and their children, but all this research had been conducted in the same sequence; that is, CMT was followed by PAT.

Harrold et al. (1992) trained two mothers in that sequence but also trained two other mothers in the sequence PAT/CMT. The dependent measures looked at mother and child behavior and compliance and affective parent/child interactions. A multiple baseline design across each pair of families was used to show that training, and not some other events, was responsible for the changes in parent/child interactions. The data showed that both treatment procedures were effective in improving parent/child interactions. Two outcomes of this research were especially noteworthy. First, PAT was as effective as CMT, something that had not been previously demonstrated. Second, most of the mothers preferred PAT, something we had noted clinically. The relevance of this was that if, in fact, parents prefer PAT and find it more natural to use than CMT, they may be more likely to use it over time, thus increasing the likelihood that the results will be more durable over time. We have found that parents trained in CMT tend to tire of it and eventually decrease their use of the procedures they have been taught.

In a systematic replication of the Harrold et al. (1992) study, Huynen and Lutzker (1992) taught four mothers PAT without teaching CMT. Generalization data were collected in several community settings and other settings within the homes in which these mothers were trained. For example, some of the generalization settings included a library, a video store, a shopping mall, and a relative's house. Within the home, training always took place in the living room or the family room. Generalization data were also collected during baths and in the kitchen.

Not only did PAT improve mother and child behavior as well as CMT had in previous research, but the generalization to many other settings was clearly evident in mother and child behavior. The social validation questionnaires completed by the mothers reported considerable satisfaction with PAT. Many of the mothers spontaneously reported that they were using PAT with their other children, thus providing anecdotal support for generalization not only across settings but across children (subjects).

The value of research across more than one individual or family lies in the demonstration that procedures or programs are effective with more than a single family or person. Although four or six families hardly represent a population, much can be gleaned by collecting repeated measure data over time as is the case in these studies. Replication demonstrates the repeated utility of the procedures, suggesting external validity and generality.

Program Evaluation

We have described four ways to evaluate the effects of an ecobehavioral model. Clinical data, while of little scientific merit, provide important and useful information for the family, the counselor, the supervisor, and the agency. Case studies allow reporting of novel effective clinical techniques. Single-case experiments allow demonstration of internal validity by showing through single-subject design that the treatment was, in fact, responsible for the behavior change. The limitation of a single-case experiment is that there is no ability to suggest generality. That is, will the treatment be effective with another individual or family? Research with more than one individual or one family allows an examination of the efficacy of procedures beyond the single-case experiment.

These four ways to evaluate outcome are very useful with any project; however, larger questions still must be asked. These questions involve an area called program evaluation. Questions of program evaluation concern the overall efficacy of the project or model. These questions may include clinical outcome issues, cost effectiveness, or social validation.

Clinical effectiveness was examined on several occasions at Project 12-Ways, the ecobehavioral approach to the treatment and prevention of child abuse and neglect. The primary program evaluation question asked about Project 12-Ways was, "Does a family receiving services from Project 12-Ways have less chance of recidivism (repeated abuse or neglect) than a family involved in child abuse or neglect in the same region who receives some other kinds of services"? In four separate analyses of this question (Lutzker & Rice, 1984; Lutzker, Wesch, & Rice, 1984; Lutzker & Rice, 1987; Wesch & Lutzker, 1991), the answer was "yes", there was lower recidivism among the families served by Project 12-Ways than among comparison groups of families from the same region who were not served by Project 12-Ways. The data generated for these comparisons came from reports of abuse or neglect collected in the Illinois Department of Children and Family Services' central office in Springfield, the state capital. Further, the Wesch and Lutzker (1991) study determined that families referred to Project 12-Ways were more problematic than the comparison group families in that they had longer histories of involvement with child protective services prior to referral than had the comparison families.

Three issues of program evaluation have been addressed by Project Ecosystems (Lutzker, Campbell, Newman, & Harrold, 1989). The first involves social validation (O'Brien, Lutzker, & Campbell, 1993). That is, how do relevant consumers of Project Ecosystems' services feel about the goals, process, and outcome of the Project? The consumers were primarily the parents of the children served, but these issues were also raised with agency personnel and other professionals who interact with Project Ecosystems' staff. Thus, separately designed questionnaires were sent to parents, agency personnel, and other professionals. The questionnaires were designed to assess what these individuals felt about the usefulness of treatment goals, the practicality and ethics of the treatment procedures, and whether these individuals perceived functional changes in behavior of the children served by Project Ecosystems.

Questions were asked not only about the clinical issues of goals, process, and outcome but also about the professionalism and humanism of the counselor staff. A five-point Likert Scale was used, with five representing the most favorable response and one representing the least favorable. On all measures, the average score was above four with the exception of the staff's knowledge about legal issues regarding developmental disabilities, which had a mean score of 3.86. We have subsequently held workshops conducted by regional center personnel to cover these legal issues. The utility of a social validation is to use it to "fine tune" any aspects of a project that may need improvement. It can also be used as a staff management tool to provide constructive feedback and praise for professional performance.

The California State Council on Developmental Disabilities conducted a cost analysis of collateral services to its vendors serving developmental disabilities. This analysis determined that, when families were seen by Project Ecosystems, collateral services are $50 less than for families not seen by Project Ecosystems. The average cost to the regional centers of service by Project Ecosystems is $1500 per family. When this is compared to $45,000 for state residential care of a child or any other more restrictive setting than the home, the cost efficiency of the project seems obvious.

In the first six years of its operation, Project Ecosystems saw over 300 families. Among those families, the placement rate of children served into more restrictive settings was less than one percent. Although we desired to create a comparison group similar to the one used with Project 12-Ways, bureaucratic impediments precluded this, but a surface analysis would suggest that this is a very desirable outcome.

Summary

We have described five ways to evaluate an ecobehavioral project, or any human service project: clinical, case study, single-subject research with one family or individual, single-subject research or group research with more than one family, and program evaluation involving social validation, cost analyses, or outcome measures. Two ecobehavioral models, Project 12-Ways and Project Ecosystems, have demonstrated the value of all five of these evaluation strategies. All clinical projects in human services should be aware of and utilize as many of these evaluation methods as possible for the sake of their consumers and their funding agents. Failure to evaluate these kinds of services should be considered an ethical flaw.

CHAPTER ELEVEN

Ethical
Issues

Awareness of ethical issues should be an aspect of any human service program. This is surely so from an ecobehavioral perspective. Issues of concern include the use of aversive procedures, the use of the experimental research designs described in Chapter 10, and issues of control inherent in the ecobehavioral approach. Also, there are questions about standards, licensing or certifying the providers of such services, and of staff management, training, and supervision.

For some time, a controversy raged within applied behavior analysis as to the ethics of using aversive procedures and whether there should be legal restrictions on using these procedures (Repp & Singh, 1990). Before the issue became internal—that is, within behavior analysis—outside pressures were brought to bear as early as 1972 *(Wyatt v. Stickney)* when government became involved in regulating behavior analysis. Restrictions were placed on certain aspects of behavioral treatment such as token economies, curtailing whole-scale token reinforcement programs within state residential facilities for populations with chronic disorders such as schizophrenia.

In the 1960s, behavioral psychology emerged from the animal laboratories and from the theoretical applications with people to real applied settings. Token reinforcement programs were shown to be effective in habilitating and rehabilitating people who had been institutionalized for years, even allowing some to return to the community. In a classic study, Paul and Lentz (1977) demonstrated that token economies were far more effective than any other contemporary practices in treating these severely disturbed populations.

Despite these dramatic successes, ethical considerations surrounded the token programs. Ultimately, it was determined that some of the components of the programs violated the civil rights of institutionalized individuals because some basic rights of these patients were being used as privileges. For example, in some of these early programs, patients earned points or tokens for learning various adaptive behaviors and participating in the psychosocial training programs offered on these units. The tokens were traded in for such reinforcers as watching television, meals, and social privileges. The courts ruled that these privileges were rights that should not be withheld for purported therapeutic purposes.

Thus, behavior analysis was thrust into considerations of some ethical issues that psychology and other human services had not encountered previously. Fortunately, the field responded with compliance to the law. The ethics of token programs were considered and adjustments were made to these programs.

No other area of human services has ever been so closely scrutinized as behavior analysis. After the issues of rights *versus* privileges in treatment surfaced and were largely resolved, behavior analysis again was scrutinized, this time for its use of aversive procedures. First, the scrutiny and attempts at control came from the outside; however, during the late 1980s and early 1990s, the issue was hotly contested within the field. Two vocal "camps" of behavior analysis emerged: one in favor of the judicious use of aversive procedures in treating seriously challenging behaviors of people with developmental disabilities and opposition to attempts to regulate these procedures, and one opposed to the use of aversive procedures and relatively unconcerned with attempts to regulate these procedures.

Although there is some disagreement as to what constitutes aversive procedures, there is a consensus that the application of painful or unpleasant procedures are considered aversive. These procedures have included contingent faradic shock, water mist, aromonic ammonia, a facial screen, and slaps. Since the 1960s, the literature has included research and clinical articles documenting various degrees of success with such procedures.

Some people from outside the field have attempted to regulate these procedures about which there has been no agreement from within as to the label "aversive." Others have suggested regulation of procedures such as time-out and response cost. Those in favor of the use of aversives present their argument in two forms: (1) It would be *unethical* to restrict or stop using aversive procedures because they have been shown to be effective, and clients, especially those who may have limited ability to advocate for themselves, have a right to effective treatment; and (2) letting nonprofessionals regulate the field restricts scientific freedom and such restrictions could lead to further restrictions that would ultimately destroy the field.

Those within behavior analysis who are opposed to the use of aversive procedures base their concerns on the notion that we should not add pain or unpleasant events to those whose lives may not be fully enriched in the first place.

Our own position tends to agree with this latter assessment and takes two additional steps (Lutzker, 1990b). First, it is our concern that there is little if any convincing evidence of the long-term or large-scale efficacy of aversive treatment procedures. The field of applied behavior analysis prides itself on its scientific approach to treating and understanding human behavior. Yet, there are no large actuarial studies showing that any particular aversive procedures have been effective, not even shock, which has been fairly widely applied. Furthermore, only a handful of studies show long-term suppression of seriously challenging behavior. Thus, the bottom line is that for a field priding itself on its empiricism, no clear data support the use of these procedures.

The second concern that we have involves scrutiny over the use of aversive procedures. To give a parent, a teacher, or other care provider an aversive technique, no matter what training in ethical guidelines may be concurrently offered, seems fraught with problems. This may be particularly so if the procedures are especially effective, at least in the short run, as is often the case with aversive procedures. There are no safeguards to keep the parent, teacher, or care provider from using the procedure for behaviors other than the one or ones on which that person may have been taught to deliver the procedure to the child. Also, no safeguards preclude the person from using the procedures with another child or individual for whom no professional training or supervision exists. For example, a parent might try the procedure on a sibling of the child in treatment.

With these concerns about the use of aversive procedures, we avoid using them on Project Ecosystems. In fact, we rarely recommend time-out because we have found planned activities training so effective. Furthermore, the concept of functional equivalence has added to our avoidance of aversive procedures. If we can teach skills incompatible with challenging behaviors and find that the challenging behaviors are concurrently reduced or eliminated, there is once again no need to contemplate using procedures that cause pain or discomfort. We would certainly want these same standards applied to ourselves or to our own children; thus, we see no reason to have differential standards for our clients.

The Ethics of Research Design

The use of the research designs described in Chapter 10 deserve mention in the context of ethical issues. The ethics of first collecting baseline data instead of entering immediately into treatment might be considered. Or the use of a multiple baseline design that protracts the baseline for one client or for a client's second behavior targeted for treatment might create an ethical dilemma.

The answer to these concerns is that failure to use simple research designs when possible might be considered more of an ethical problem than not to use these designs. Having confidence in treatment procedures because of the use of research designs is, in fact, the ethical route that more clinicians should take. The data gleaned from these designs allow them to be published and replicated, benefiting more than one client. The data also allow an ability to share and monitor progress or lack of it with family members or supervisory personnel. Empiricizing treatment makes it replicable and allows it to be tested and revised for each individual.

From its beginning in the mid-1960s, critics of behavior analysis have been concerned about procedures that appeared to be mechanical, contrived, and manipulative, thus "controlling." The critics were answered that the success of some of these procedures with challenging behaviors that were previously untreatable was testimony to the need to use them, and that once new skills were taught, the natural environment would be likely to maintain the new behaviors, thus requiring less structured procedures such as token reinforcement.

In many cases these answers are sufficient. But the critics were also right in some ways. For example, although behavior analysis has documented considerable success with very difficult populations, such as children with autism, research and experience over the years has shown that when we have taught language to these children, it was rather mechanical in its effect and seldom generative or spontaneous. Thus, research in recent years in teaching language to children with autism (Charlop, Kurtz, & Casey, 1990) has moved toward using more natural teaching environments and natural contingencies. This, in turn, has produced more natural language and affect by the children.

It is our experience with Project Ecosystems that families tire easily with token reinforcement programs, largely because of their artificiality. We have overcome this by using token programs sparingly to begin with and by fading them out quickly, using many of the principles in planned activities training to prevent them from becoming problems that necessitate a token reinforcement program.

It is our concerted opinion that the ecobehavioral approach provides some answers to previous ethical concerns about applied behavior analysis. In explicating this approach in Chapter 1, we noted that ecobehavioral means, in part, biobehavioral and promotes generality. These are concerns that all programs should address. Working with developmental disabilities, any professionals or agencies are necessarily involved in biobehavioral issues. Thus, to conduct a treatment program without involvement with medical personnel would delimit any clear treatment progress. Similarly, we feel that in-home, in-situ approaches are more likely to produce generalization over time (durability of treatment effects). Also, active programming for generalization of all treatment programs should be a prerequisite in any project. These are ethical issues about which we believe the fields of applied behavior analysis and ecobehavioral analysis have shown leadership, and we question the ethics of clinic-based and narrow focus programs within behavior analysis and other areas of psychology that lack these components.

Staff training was the topic of Chapter 9. But, it also deserves mention in a discussion of ethics. Training and supervision is at the core of an ethical human service. There should be confidence that the staff delivering any service has had a theoretical background strongly reinforced with "hands-on" training and frequent direct and indirect supervision. Considerable research has shown that performance-based skills, such as teaching behavior management techniques to parents, must be taught directly using modeling, role-playing, and feedback. Such training should always include performance criteria so the teacher knows when the student is actually trained. Also, such training should include written performance so the teacher knows that the student is also aware of the theoretical background and legal and ethical issues involved in treatment. For example, in teaching a Project Ecosystems counselor how to conduct a time-out protocol, that counselor would first read about how to do it, read about the legal and ethical issues in implementing a time-out program, and then be required to pass a written test to a 90 percent criterion before experiencing the hands-on training for conducting a time-out protocol.

Supervision should take two forms, as it does on Project Ecosystems. Regular meetings occur between Project Ecosystems' counselors and their supervisors. In these meetings, each case is discussed and data are shared from the families served by the project. For example, a counselor might present the supervisor with data on child compliance after the mother has received planned activities training. The supervisor might also assign the counselor reading. This reading might include treatment, research, or an overview of a disorder such as ADHD. The supervisor might also review videotapes of the PAT that had been conducted in the home and offer suggestions on how to improve the training.

The other form of supervision is direct observation of the counselor. This takes the form of the supervisor accompanying the counselor on a home visit after the counselor has apprised the family of the supervisor's intentions and received the family's permission for the supervisory visit. It is our strong belief that these two forms of supervision are essential in maintaining quality control on the project and that any mental health or other human service agency that does not apply a similar model of supervision should be open for serious question.

Licensure and Certification

As there has recently been a debate within the field of behavior analysis about use of aversive procedures, there has been a longer yet less acrimonious debate as to whether behavior analysis should license or certify professionals or programs specifically in behavior analysis. These currently fall within the broader licensure and certification of psychology. One of the reasons for this concern is that many well-qualified practitioners of behavior analysis, especially those working in developmental disabilities, have subdoctoral, usually masters-level, degrees. Most states no longer recognize subdoctoral professionals for licensing as psychologists. Further, the skills and academic background for practicing psychology are different from those needed to work in behavior analysis and developmental disabilities.

Only one state, Florida, has successfully created and implemented a statewide, recognized certification procedure for behavior analysts working in developmental disabilities. Subdoctoral professionals are able to deliver services for Project Ecosystems because they are supervised by a licensed psychologist and the vendorization of Project Ecosystems is under the authority of the state Department of Developmental Services, not the state Psychology Examining Committee.

Whether behavior analysts in other states will be successful in following Florida's lead remains an empirical issue. It does appear that the Association for Behavior Analysis will go forward with accrediting graduate programs in behavior analysis, but it is unclear what impact such accreditation might have. The presumed value in accreditation, licensure, or certification is in protecting or at least informing consumers about service providers. Issues remain as to the best means for assessing and maintaining competency in such a field.

We believe that the ecobehavioral model described in this book, certainly including the means of evaluation described in Chapter 10, goes a long way toward an ethical approach to consumer protection.

Finally, staff training and supervision requires understanding and awareness of state-of-the-art research in the field. Attendance at regional conferences and inviting speakers and consultants to staff meetings are important aspects of quality control, as is assigning journals and other readings.

Keeping abreast of current professional developments in any field relates to the ethical need to keep any program dynamic. Our ecobehavioral model was born in part out of experience and recognition that applied behavior analysis with children had worn thin, that it lacked creativity and ignored broad issues that needed attention if we were to be truly effective with families with serious disorders (Lutzker, 1992). Similarly, our model has changed as a function of others' research and our own data and observations of weaknesses. Today's ecobehavioral model is different from yesterday's, and we are sure that tomorrow's will be different too. We believe that this dynamic is a critical aspect of ethical concern in work in human services.

Conclusions

The ecobehavioral model has been shown to be effective in treating families involved in child abuse and neglect in rural southern Illinois. It has been shown to be effective with families with children who have developmental disabilities in southern California. We have used adaptations of the model when working in residential facilities treating chronic schizophrenia and head injury (Lutzker, 1993b). It is our hope that this empirical, broad-based, multifaceted approach can be replicated in child abuse and neglect, developmental disabilities, and a wider range of human problems in a variety of other communities and settings.

References

Allen, K. E., Hart, B. M., Buell, J. S., Harris, F. R., & Wolf, M. M. (1964). Effects of social reinforcement on isolate behavior of a nursery school child. In L. Ullman, and L. Krasner (eds.), *Case studies in behavior modification.* (pp. 307–312). New York: Holt, Rinehart & Winston.

Azrin, N. H., & Foxx, R. M. (1974). *Toilet training in less than a day.* New York: Simon & Schuster.

Azrin, N. H., Naster, B. J., & Jones, J. R. (1973). Reciprocity counseling: A rapid learning-based procedure for marital counseling. *Behaviour Research and Therapy, 11,* 365–383.

Baker, B. L. (1984). Interventions with families with young handicapped children. In J. Blacher (ed.), *Severely handicapped young children and their families* (pp. 319–375). Orlando, FL: Academic Press.

Bakken, H., Miltenberger, R. G., & Schauss, S. (1993). Teaching parents with mental retardation: Knowledge versus skills. *American Journal on Mental Retardation, 97,* 405–417.

Bandura, A. (1969). *Principles of behavior modification*. New York: Holt, Rinehart & Winston.

Barone, V. J., Greene, B. F., & Lutzker, J. R. (1986). Home safety with families being treated for child abuse and neglect. *Behavior Modification, 10,* 93–114.

Beale, I. L., Smith, O. A., & Webster, D. M. (1993). Effects of chlorpromazine and thioridazine on discrimination learning in children with mental retardation. *Journal of Developmental and Physical Disabilities, 5,* 43–54.

Beck, A. T., & Beamesderfer, A. (1974). Assessment of depression: The Depression inventory. In P. Pichot (ed.), *Modern problems in pharmacopsychiatry* (pp. 151–169). Basel, Switzerland: S. Karger.

Beckman, P. (1991). Comparison of mothers' and fathers' perceptions of the effect of young children with and without developmental disabilities. *American Journal on Mental Retardation, 95,* 585–595.

Bernal, M. E., Klinnert, M. D., & Schultz, L. A. (1980). Outcome evaluation of behavioral parent training and client-centered parent counseling for children with conduct problems. *Journal of Applied Behavior Analysis, 13,* 677–691.

Bigelow, K. M., Huynen, K. B., & Lutzker, J. R. (1993). Using a changing criterion design to teach fire escape to a child with developmental disabilities. *Journal of Developmental and Physical Disabilities, 5,* 121–128.

Biglan, A. (1989). A contextual approach to the clinical treatment of parental distress. In G. H. S. Singer and L. K. Irvin (eds.), *Support for caregiving families: Enabling positive adaptation to disability* (pp. 299–311). Baltimore: Paul H. Brookes.

Black, M. M., Molaison, V. A., & Smull, M. W. (1990). Families caring for young adults with mental retardation. Service needs and urgency of community living requests. *American Journal on Mental Retardation, 95,* 32–39.

Blount, R. L., Dahlquist, L. M., Baer, R. A., & Wuori, D. (1984). A brief effective method for teaching children to swallow pills. *Behavior Therapy, 15,* 381–387.

Borck, L. E., & Fawcett, S. B. (1982). *Learning counseling and problem-solving skills*. New York: Haworth.

Breslau, N., & Prabucki, K. (1987). Siblings of disabled children: Effects of chronic stress in the family. *Archives of General Psychiatry, 44,* 1040–1046.

Brown, K. M., Willis, B. S., & Reid, D. H. (1981). Differential effects of supervisor feedback and feedback plus approval on institutional staff performance. *Journal of Organizational Behavior Management, 3,* 57–68.

Burg, M. M., Reid, D. H., & Lattimore, J. (1979). Use of a self-recording and supervision program to change institutional staff behavior. *Journal of Applied Behavior Analysis, 12,* 363–375.

Campbell, R. V., & Lutzker, J. R. (1993). Using functional equivalence training to reduce severe challenging behavior. *Journal of Developmental and Physical Disabilities, 5,* 203–216.

Campbell, R. V., O'Brien S., Bickett, A., & Lutzker, J. R. (1983). In-home parent-training, treatment of migraine headaches, and marital counseling as an ecobehavioral approach to prevent child abuse. *Journal of Behavior Therapy and Experimental Psychiatry, 14,* 147–154.

Charlop, M. H., Kurtz, P. F., & Casey, F. G. (1990). Using aberrant behaviors as reinforcers for autistic children. *Journal of Applied Behavior Analysis, 23,* 163–181.

Creer, T. L. (1970). The use of time-out from positive reinforcement procedures with asthmatic children. *Journal of Psychosomatic Research, 14,* 117–120.

Delgado, L. E., & Lutzker, J. R. (1988). Training young parents to identify and report their children's illnesses. *Journal of Applied Behavior Analysis, 21,* 311–319.

Dyson, L. L. (1991). Families of young children with handicaps: Parental stress and family functioning. *American Journal on Mental Retardation, 95,* 623–629.

Forehand, R. L. (1986). Parental positive reinforcement with deviant children: Does it make a difference? *Child and Family Behavior Therapy, 8,* 19–25.

Forehand, R. L., & McMahon, R. J. (1981). *Helping the noncompliant child: A clinician's guide to parent training.* New York: Guilford.

Forehand, R. L., & Wierson, M. (1993). The role of developmental factors in planning behavioral interventions for children: Disruptive behavior as an example. *Behavior Therapy, 24,* 117–141.

Goddard, H. H. (1912). *The Kallikak family: A study in the heredity of feeblemindedness.* New York: MacMillan.

Gordon, T. (1975). *Parent effectiveness training.* New York: Peter H. Wyden.

Greene, B. F., Willis, B. F., Levy, R., & Bailey, J. S. (1978). Measuring client gains from staff-implemented programs. *Journal of Applied Behavior Analysis, 11,* 395–412.

Gregg, J., & Williamson, B. (1992). Practical alternatives to traditional intervention. *The Behavior Therapist, 15,* 165–167.

Griest, D. L., Forehand, R., Rogers, T., Breiner, J., Furey, W., & Williams, C. A. (1982). Effects of parent enhancement therapy on the treatment, outcome, and generalization of a parent training program. *Behaviour Research and Therapy, 20,* 429–436.

Halvorsen, A. T., Doering, K., Farron-Davis, F., Usilton, R., & Sailor, N. (1989). The role of parents and family members in planning severely disabled students' transitions from school. In G. H. S. Singer and L. K. Irvin (eds.), *Support for caregiving families: Enabling positive adaptation to disability* (pp. 253–268). Baltimore: Paul H. Brookes.

Haring, T. G., & Kennedy, G. H. (1990). Contextual control of problem behavior in students with severe disabilities. *Journal of Applied Behavior Analysis, 23,* 235–243.

Harrold, M., Lutzker, J. R., Campbell, R. V., & Touchette, P. E. (1992). Project Ecosystems: An ecobehavioral approach to families with children with developmental disabilities. *Journal of Developmental and Physical Disabilities, 4,* 1–14.

Hart, B. M., & Risley, T. R. (1975). Incidental teaching of language in the preschool. *Journal of Applied Behavior Analysis, 8,* 411–420.

Hutchins, V. L., & McPherson, M. (1991). National agenda for children with special health needs: Social policy for the 1990s through the 21st century. *American Psychologist, 46,* 141–143.

Huynen, K. B., & Lutzker, J. R. (May 25–28, 1992). Planned activities training for families: An Aussie miracle? Paper presented at the 15th Annual Convention of the Association for Behavior Analysis, San Francisco, CA.

Jacobson, E. (1938). *Progressive relaxation.* Chicago: University of Chicago Press.

Katz, R. C., & Lutzker, J. R. (1980). A comparison of three methods for training timeout. *Behavior Research of Severe Developmental Disabilities, 1,* 123–130.

Kazdin, A. E. (1982). *Single-case research designs: Methods for clinical and applied settings.* New York: Oxford University Press.

Kempe, C. H., Silverman, F. N., Steele, B. F., Droegemueller, N., & Silver, H. K.

(1962). The battered-child syndrome. *Journal of the American Medical Association, 181,* 105–112.

Kiesel, K. B., Lutzker, J. R., & Campbell, R. V. (1989). Behavioral relaxation training to reduce hyperventilation and seizures in a profoundly retarded epileptic child. *Journal of the Multihandicapped Person, 2,* 179–190.

Kissel, R. C., Whitman, T. L., & Reid, D. H. (1983). An institutional staff training and self-management program for developing multiple self-care skills in severely/profoundly retarded individuals. *Journal of Applied Behavior Analysis, 16,* 395–415.

Krauss, M. W. (1993). Child-related and parenting stress: Similarities and differences between mothers and fathers of children with disabilities. *American Journal on Mental Retardation, 97,* 393–403.

Lowe, K., & Lutzker, J. R. (1979). Increasing compliance to a medical regimen in a juvenile diabetic. *Behavior Therapy, 10,* 57–64.

Lutzker, J. R. (1984). Project 12-Ways: Treating child abuse and neglect from an ecobehavioral perspective. In R. F. Dangel and R. A. Polster (eds.), *Parent training: Foundations of research and practice* (pp. 260–291). New York: Guilford.

Lutzker, J. R. (1990a). Behavioral treatment of child neglect. *Behavior Modification, 14,* 301–315.

Lutzker, J. R. (1990b). "Damn It, Burris, I'm not a product of Walden Two," or who's controlling the controllers? In A. Repp and N. Singh (eds.), *Severe behavior problems in developmental disabilities: Issues in nonaversive therapy* (pp. 495–501). Sycamore, IL: Sycamore.

Lutzker, J. R. (1992). Developmental disabilities and child abuse and neglect: The ecobehavioral imperative. *Behaviour Change, 9,* 149–156.

Lutzker, J. R. (1993a). Behavior analysis for developmental disabilities: The stages of efficacy and comparative treatments. In T. R. Giles (ed.), *Handbook of effective psychotherapy.* (pp. 89–106). New York: Plenum.

Lutzker, J. R. (1993b, February 18–20). *Engagement: Another name for stimulus control; treating families; head injury; developmental disabilities.* Invited address at the 12th Annual Conference of the Northern California Association for Behavior Analysis, Oakland, CA.

Lutzker, J. R., Campbell, R. V., Newman, M. R., & Harrold, M. (1989). Ecobehavioral interventions for abusive, neglectful, and high-risk families. In G. H. S. Singer, and L. K. Irvin (eds.). *Support for caregiving families: Enabling positive adaptation to disability* (pp. 313–326). Baltimore: Paul H. Brookes

Lutzker, J. R., & Martin, J. A. (1981). *Behavior Change.* Pacific Grove, CA: Brooks/Cole.

Lutzker, J. R., McGimsey, J. F., McRae, S., & Campbell, R. V. (1983). Behavioral parent training: There's so much more to do. *The Behavior Therapist, 6,* 110–112.

Lutzker, J. R., Megson, D. A., Webb, M. E., & Dachman, R. S. (1985). Validating and training adult-child interaction skills to professionals and to parents indicated for child abuse and neglect. *Journal of Child and Adolescent Psychotherapy, 2,* 91–104.

Lutzker, J. R., & Rice, J. M. (1984). Project 12-Ways: Measuring outcome of a large-scale in-home service for the treatment and prevention of child abuse and neglect. *Child Abuse and Neglect: The International Journal, 8,* 519–524.

Lutzker, J. R., & Rice, J. M. (1987). Using recidivism data to evaluate Project 12-Ways: An ecobehavioral approach to the treatment and prevention of child abuse and neglect. *Journal of Family Violence, 2,* 283–290.

Lutzker, J. R., Touchette, P. E., & Campbell, R. V. (1988). Parental positive reinforcement might make a difference: A rejoinder to Forehand. *Child and Family Behavior Therapy, 10,* 25–33.

Lutzker, J. R., Wesch, D., & Rice, J. M. (1984). A review of Project 12-Ways: An ecobehavioral approach to the treatment and prevention of child abuse and neglect. *Advances in Behaviour Research and Therapy, 6,* 63–73.

Lutzker, S. Z., Lutzker, J. R., Braunling-McMorrow, D., & Eddleman, J. (1987). Prompting to increase mother-baby stimulation with single mothers. *Journal of Child and Adolescent Psychotherapy, 4,* 3–12.

McEachin, J. J., Smith, T., & Lovaas, O. I. (1993). Long-term outcome for children with autism who received early intensive behavioral treatment. *American Journal on Mental Retardation, 97,* 359–372.

McGimsey, J. F. (1987). Training child abuse professionals in behavior management and consultation: The effects on mediators (parents) and consumers (children). Unpublished dissertation. Southern Illinois University.

Meinhold, P. M., & Mulick, J. A. (1990). Counter-habilitative contingencies in institutions for people with mental retardation: Ecological and regulatory influences. *Mental Retardation, 28,* 67–76.

Nedelman, D., & Salzbacher, S. I. (1972). Dicky at 13 years of age: A long-term success following early application of operant conditioning procedures. In G. Semb (ed.) *Behavior analysis and education* (pp. 3–10) Lawrence, KS: University of Kansas.

Newman, M. R. (1989). Training trainers: Examining generalization in teaching problem-solving and child management skills. Unpublished dissertation. California School of Professionals, Los Angeles.

Nezu, C. M., Nezu, A. M., & Gill-Weiss, M. J. (1992). *Psychopathology in persons with mental retardation: Clinical guidelines for assessment and treatment.* Champaign, IL: Research Press.

O'Brien, M. P., Lutzker, J. R., & Campbell, R. V. (1993). Consumer evaluation of an ecobehavioral program for families with children with developmental disabilities. *Journal of Mental Health Administration, 20,* 278–284.

O'Neill, R. E., Horner, R. H., Albin, R. W., Storey, K., & Sprague, J. R. (1990). *Functional assessment of problem behaviors: a practical assessment guide.* Sycamore, IL: Sycamore.

Paul, G. L. & Lentz, R. S. (1977). *Psychosocial treatment of chronic mental patients.* Cambridge, MA: Harvard University Press.

Pelham, W. E., & Hinshaw, S. P. (1992). Behavioral intervention for attention deficit-hyperactive disorder. In S. M. Turner, K. S. Calhoun, and H. E. Adams (eds.), *Handbook of clinical behavior therapy,* 2nd edition. (pp. 259–283). New York: Wiley.

Pomerleau, O. F. (1979). Behavioral medicine: The contribution of the experimental analysis of behavior to medical care. *American Psychologist, 34,* 654–663.

Poppen, R. (1988). *Behavioral relaxation training and assessment.* New York: Pergamon.

Prinz, R. J. (1992). Overview of behavioural family interventions with children: Achievements, limitations, and challenges. *Behaviour Change, 9,* 120–125.

Quilitch, H. R. (1975). A comparison of three staff management procedures. *Journal of Applied Behavior Analysis, 8,* 59–66.

Repp, A. C., & Singh, N. N. (1990). *Perspectives on the use of nonaversive interventions for persons with developmental disabilities*. Sycamore, IL: Sycamore.

Rice, J. M., & Lutzker, J. R. (1984). Reducing noncompliance to follow-up appointment-keeping at a family practice center. *Journal of Applied Behavior Analysis, 17*, 303–311.

Ricketts, R. W., Ellis, C. R., Singh, Y. N., & Singh, N. H. (1993). Opoid antagonists. II. Clinical effects in the treatment of self-injury in individuals with developmental disabilities. *Journal of Developmental and Physical Disabilities, 5*, 17–27.

Roberts, R. R., & Magrab, P. R. (1991). Psychologists' role in a family-centered approach to practice, training, and research with young children. *American Psychologist, 46*, 144–148.

Roberts, R. R., Wasik, R. H., Casto, G., & Ramey, C. T. (1991). Family support in the home: Programs, policy, and social change. *American Psychologist, 46*, 131–137.

Rogers-Warren, A., & Warren, S. F. (1977). *Ecological perspectives in behavior analysis*. Baltimore: University Park Press.

Russo, D. C., & Varni, J. W. (1982). *Behavioral pediatrics: Research and practice*. New York: Plenum.

Sallis, J. F. (1983). Aggressive behaviors of children: A review of behavioral interventions and future directions. *Education and Treatment of Children, 6*, 175–191.

Sanders, M. R. (1992). Enhancing the impact of behavioural family intervention with children: Emerging perspectives. *Behaviour Change, 9*, 115–119.

Sanders, M. R., & Dadds, M. R. (1982). The effects of planned activities and child management training: An analysis of setting generality. *Behavior Therapy, 13*, 1–11.

Sanders, M. R., & Dadds, M. R. (1987). *Planned activities training*. Brisbane: University of Queensland Press.

Sanders, M. R., & Dadds, M. R. (1993). *Behavioral family intervention*. Needham Heights, MA: Allyn & Bacon.

Sanders, M. R., & Markie-Dadds, C. (1992). Toward a technology of prevention of disruptive behavior disorders: The role of behavioral family intervention. *Behaviour Change, 9*, 186–200.

Sarber, R. E., Halasz, M. M., Messmer, M. C., Bickett, A. D., & Lutzker, J. R., (1983). Teaching menu planning and grocery shopping skills to a mentally retarded mother. *Mental Retardation, 21*, 101–106.

Schilling, D. J., & Poppen, R. (1983). Behavioral relaxation training and assessment. *Journal of Behavior Therapy and Experimental Psychiatry, 14*, 99–107.

Singer, G. H. S., & Irvin, L. K. (1989). Family caregiving, stress, and support. In G. H. S. Singer and L. K. Irvin (eds.), *Support for caregiving families: Enabling positive adaptation to disability* (pp. 3–25). Baltimore: Paul H. Brookes.

Singer, G. H. S., Irvine, A. B., & Irvin, L. K. (1989). Expanding the focus of behavioral parent-training: A contextual approach. In G. H. S. Singer and L. K. Irvin (eds.), *Support for caregiving families: Enabling positive adaptation to disability* (pp. 85–102). Baltimore: Paul H. Brookes.

Singh, Y. N., Ricketts, R. W., Ellis, C. R., & Singh, W. H. (1993). Opoid antagonists. I: Pharmacology and rationale for use in treating self-injury. *Journal of Developmental and Physical Disabilities, 5*, 5–15.

Solnick, J. V., Rincover, A., & Peterson, C. P. (1977). Some determinants of the reinforcing and punishing effects of timeout. *Journal of Applied Behavior Analysis, 10*, 415–424.

Stokes, T. K., & Baer, D. M. (1977). An implicit technology of generalization. *Journal of Applied Behavior Analysis, 10,* 349–367.

Summers, J. A., Behr, S. K., & Turnbull, A. P. (1989). Positive adaptation and coping strengths of families who have children with disabilities. In G. H. S. Singer and L. K. Irvin (eds.), *Support for caregiving families: Enabling positive adaptation to disability* (pp. 27–40). Baltimore: Paul H. Brookes.

Szykula, S. A., Fleischman, M. J., & Shilton, P. E. (1982). Implementing a family therapy program in a community: Relevant issues on one promising program for families in conflict. *Behavioral Counseling Quarterly, 2,* 67–68.

Taylor, D. V., Sandman, C. A., Touchette, P. E., Hetrick, W. P., & Barron, J. L. (1993). Naltrexone improves learning and attention in self-injurious individuals with developmental disabilities. *Journal of Developmental and Physical Disabilities, 5,* 29–41.

Taylor, S. J., Knoll, J. A., Lehr, S., & Walker, P. M. (1989). Families for all children: Value-based services for children with disabilities and their families. In. G. H. S. Singer and L. K. Irvin (eds.), *Support for caregiving families: Enabling positive adaptation to disability* (pp. 41–54). Baltimore: Paul H. Brookes.

Tertinger, D., Greene, B. F., & Lutzker, J. R. (1984). Home safety: Development and validation of one component of an ecobehavioral treatment program for abused and neglected children. *Journal of Applied Behavior Analysis, 17,* 159–174.

Tertinger, D., Greene, B. F., & Lutzker, J. R. (1988). Home accident prevention inventory. In M. Hersen and A. S. Bellack (eds.), *Dictionary of behavioral assessment techniques* (pp. 246–248). New York: Pergamon.

Touchette, P. E., McDonald, R., & Langer, S. (1985). A scatterplot for discovering stimulus control of a problem behavior. *Journal of Applied Behavior Analysis, 18,* 343–351.

Turnbull, A. P., & Turnbull, H. R. T. III. (1990). *Families, professionals, and exceptionality: A special partnership.* Columbus, OH: Merrill.

Twardosz, S., Weddle, K., Borden, L., & Stevens, E. (1986). A comparison of three methods of preparing children for surgery. *Behavior Therapy, 17,* 14–25.

Varni, J. W., & Deitrich, S. L. (1981). Behavioral pediatrics: Towards a reconceptualization. *Behavioral Medicine Update, 3,* 5–7.

Wahler, R. S., & Fox, J. J. (1980). Setting events in applied behavior analysis: Toward a conceptual and methodological expansion. *Journal of Applied Behavior Analysis, 14,* 327–338.

Warren, F., & Warren, S. H. (1989). The role of parents in creating and maintaining quality family support services. In G. H. S. Singer and L. K. Irvin (eds.), *Support for caregiving families: Enabling positive adaptation to disability* (pp. 55–68). Baltimore: Paul H. Brookes.

Watson-Perczel, M., Lutzker, J. R., Greene, B. F., & McGimpsey, B. J. (1988). Assessment and modification of home cleanliness among families adjudicated for child neglect. *Behavior Modification, 12,* 57–81.

Weisner, T. S., Beizer, L., & Stolze, L. (1991). Religion and families of children with developmental delays. *American Journal of Mental Retardation, 95,* 647–662.

Wesch, D., & Lutzker, J. R. (1991). A comprehensive evaluation of Project 12-Ways: An ecobehavioral program for treating and preventing child abuse and neglect. *Journal of Family Violence,* 17–35.

Winett, R., & Winkler, R. (1972). Current behavior modification in the classroom: Be still, quiet, and docile. *Journal of Applied Behavior Analysis, 5,* 499–504.

Wolf, M. M., Risley, T. R., & Mees, H. (1964). Application of operant conditioning procedures to the behavior problems of an autistic child. *Behaviour Research and Therapy, 1,* 305–312.

Wyatt v. *Stickney,* 344 F. Supp. 373, 344 F. Supp. 387 (M.D. Ala 1972).

Ziarnick, J. P., & Bernstein, G. S. (1982). A critical examination of the effect of in-service training on staff performance. *Mental Retardation, 20,* 109–114.

Zigler, E., Hodapp, R. M., & Edison, M. R. (1990). From theory to practice in the care and education of mentally retarded individuals. *American Journal of Mental Retardation, 95,* 1–12.

Author Index

Subject Index